LESTER PIGGOTT

THE PICTORIAL BIOGRAPHY

LESTER PIGGOTT

THE PICTORIAL BIOGRAPHY

JULIAN WILSON

Macdonald
Queen Anne Press

To Iris and Keith Piggott, who created a genius.

A Queen Anne Press BOOK

First published in hardback in Great Britain in 1985 by
Queen Anne Press, a division of
Macdonald & Co (Publishers) Ltd
Greater London House, Hampstead Road,
London NW1 7QX
This edition first published in paperback in 1986 by
Queen Anne Press.

A BPCC plc Company

Cover photographs: Gerry Cranham

British Library Cataloguing in Publication Data

Wilson, Julian
Lester Piggott: the pictorial biography
1. Piggott, Lester – Portraits, etc.
2. Jockeys – Great Britain – Biography
I. Title
798.4'3'0924 SF336.P5

ISBN 0-356-12033-3

ISBN 0-356-12579-3 Pbk

Typeset by Sios Limited, London NW6

Reproduced, printed and bound in Great Britain by
R J Acford, Chichester, Sussex.

CONTENTS

BORN TO BE CHAMPION

Lester Keith Piggott was born and bred to ride: there was no alternative. His pedigree is the human equivalent to that of the finest thoroughbred. His father, Keith, was a top-class steeplechase jockey and Grand National winning trainer; his jockey grandfather, Ernie, won three Grand Nationals; and his mother, Iris, won the Newmarket Town Plate – in those days the only race open to women riders.

The nineteenth century Piggotts were Cheshire farmers; great-grandfather, Tom Piggott, farmed on a large scale near Nantwich. There were three sons – Ernie, Charlie and Jack. All were hard riders to hounds in what was then, long before the advent of motorways, some of England's finest hunting country. Tom's was a 'dealing' yard, and amongst the family's clients was a youthful Winston Churchill.

The family's fortunes met with a crisis when Tom Piggott's entire livestock was wiped out by an epidemic of foot and mouth disease. The destitute farmer had no option but to relinquish farming and seek a new livelihood. Eventually he became landlord and owner of the Crown Hotel, Nantwich.

His son Ernie, meanwhile, became a professional jockey, and was very soon one of the outstanding riders in England, France and Belgium. In 1910 he collected the first of three Champion Jockey titles, and two years later won the Grand National on Jerry M. In 1918 he won a war-time Grand National at Gatwick on Poethlyn, and the following year won the real thing at Aintree on the same horse. Both Jerry M and Poethlyn carried 12st 7lbs at Aintree – the only horses this century to win under the maximum weight.

In the twenties, Ernie Piggott became a trainer at Wantage, while his brother Charlie trained at Cheltenham. In 1939, Charlie won the Champion Hurdle with a mare

The face like a 'well-kept grave'. The rigours of self-discipline and deprivation have taken their toll; bones and muscles ache; and thin silk colours provide scant protection against cold autumn winds. But still the demon drove him on.

Gerry Cranham

Two of the finest Grand National winners of all time, both ridden by Ernie Piggott. The massive Jerry M won in 1912, having been off-the-course for two years. Poethlyn won a war-time substitute at Gatwick in 1918, and the first post-war National the following year.
W.W. Rouch

OPPOSITE PAGE. BOTTOM LEFT:
Fred Archer (1857-1886), the greatest jockey of the nineteenth century, with whom Piggott shares so many characteristics.
BBC Hulton Picture Library

BOTTOM RIGHT:
Sir Gordon Richards (1904-   ), the most popular jockey in racing history, who rode 4,870 winners from 21,843 mounts in Britain. Bassano Ltd

called African Sister, ridden by Lester's father, Keith. Keith had become one of the finest National Hunt jockeys of the pre-war period, with other major successes including the Grand Sefton Chase and Welsh Grand National.

He had a ruthless streak and a keen disregard for most amateur riders. The story is told that one day, in a selling steeplechase at Gatwick, Keith was tailed off with a fence to jump, and about to pull up, when he saw behind him an amateur riding determinedly for the last fence. Keith rode him ruthlessly into the wings and the amateur plus mount crashed into a tangled heap.

Later, in the dressing room, the amateur came up to Keith and demanded angrily,

'What was that for?'

'Just keeping in practice!' said Keith.

Keith, having ridden over 500 winners, became a

trainer in 1945, and his greatest triumph was to win the Grand National with the 66-1 shot Ayala, owned by 'Teasie Weasie' Raymond, in 1963.

Lester's mother Iris was a fine rider, and strong personality. Her father, Fred Rickaby, was first jockey to Lord Derby in the 1890s, and won the Oaks on Canterbury Pilgrim. Iris's brother, also christened Fred, emulated his father in becoming stable jockey to Lord Derby and won the 1,000 Guineas four times. His son, Bill Rickaby, became one of the most popular flat race jockeys of the post-war era until his retirement in 1968.

A glance at Lester's family tree reveals other great racing names, like Tom Cannon, who rode his first winner at the age of nine, and the legendary John Day.

So Lester Piggott, born on 5 November 1935, and

Lester takes on his father at Keith's favourite game. Even now, at eighty-one, Keith enjoys nothing more than a game of draughts, although Iris, engrossed here in the Western Daily Mail, *has never learned to play!* Photo Source/Fox

Champion Apprentice at the age of fourteen. Lester, at the end of his third season, which yielded fifty-two winners. The Press speculated that the following year he would 'Earn more than a Cabinet Minister. . . £5,000!' Photo Source/Keystone

At the age of fifteen, fan mail was a diverting novelty. In later life, it entailed shoals of pre-signed photographs, a full-time secretary and as many autographs each day as his fingers could bear to sign.
Photo Source/Fox

OPPOSITE PAGE:
Twelve years old and the future clearly defined! The previous week at unfashionable Haydock Park, L. Piggott weighing barely six stone, had ridden the first of over 5,000 winners. Photo Source/Keystone

destined to be an only child, had a 'mixed' racing pedigree: National Hunt on his father's side and Flat on his mother's. At one stage, it looked as though the man who was to become probably the greatest flat jockey of all time was destined to follow his father into the jumping game!

Lester sat on his first pony at the age of four. It was a little New Forest pony, called Brandy – and he was well named! Keith Piggott was thrown four times while he was breaking in the little fire-brand, and Iris was far from convinced he was the ideal conveyance for her only son. Lester was finally legged up – and might have been riding all his life.

Within a couple of years Lester was competing in the local gymkhanas against much older boys. His problem was that being so small he could never get back on a horse in obstacle races! At the age of seven Lester was riding a racehorse, and before long was leading Keith's string of jumpers in schooling over hurdles.

Announcing 3rd Edition of
The WONDER SYSTEM OF 1948
SENT FREE!
If you promise SECRECY
METHOD EVER DEVISED
LATEST CONVERTS:
A Few More!
EVER INVENTED
£2
£3/10/-
SOLUTIONS FOR THE BIG PRIZE PUZZLES
The WINNER
FOOTBALL FORECASTS THAT WIN THE POOLS
BEST FOR YORK 4-DAY RACING FESTIVAL
Great Ebor Handicap Special
"GIMCRACK" & NUNTHORPE NAPS
By "THE BARD"
YORK
'THE BARD'S' SELECTIONS
STARDOM 100-8
SASKIA 100-30 SEALED ORDERS 3-1
LACOVEDIS 11-4 WOODBURN 5-2
The WINNER
WEEK-END SPECIAL
RIPON, WORCESTER, BRIGHTON & LEWES
1/-
AT ALL NEWSAGENTS

The Age of Convention. Lester aged fifteen, with perfect seat and ideal length of leg. It was his further six inches growth that created the need to adopt his inimitable balancing act. Technically his style was never more correct than at this time. Note the now defunct stands of Hurst Park, closed for development in 1962.

Sport & General

The 'Boy Wonder' at 16 already twice Champion Apprentice and about to enjoy the first of 32 Derby rides. But father Keith was still 'The Boss'. The late Dominic Forte was Lester's fellow apprentice.

Photo Source/Fox

Between 6.30 a.m. and 8.30 a.m. he was leading the life of a stable lad – grooming, mucking out and riding out – and for the rest of the day the normal life of a schoolboy. Going to school – St Alfred's, Wantage – was a routine that Lester suffered with rueful resignation.

'I didn't really know what school was for, except that you had to go to it,' he reflects.

He found it merely a tiresome interruption to being with horses, and his academic record reflected that. He was considered slow, and not good at anything except football and cricket. How much he was inhibited by his partial deafness is hard to determine. Lester has never been one for excuses, or even for explanations. As a child he was always a 'loner'. When not with horses he would play on his own, and preferred his own company.

His father was a hard task-master from a tough school.

'He knew his stuff, and I tried to please him because I knew he knew his stuff,' Lester once said. 'I wanted to be good and I was ready to take it from him.'

Many onlookers, however, felt that Keith was unduly hard on Lester, encouraging his son to run before he could walk. But Lester was a natural, with marvellous hands, and no fear.

Nowadays a boy must be sixteen years old before he can ride in a race; in the forties and fifties a boy could be apprenticed at the age of twelve. Lester had shown such skill and determination on the gallops that Keith took out an apprentice's licence for his son on his twelfth birthday. His schooling was re-directed from St Alfred's to private tuition with a Miss Westlake at Lambourn, two or three days a week.

Within two weeks of the start of the new season of 1948, Lester had his first ride, on a filly called The Chase in a race at Salisbury carrying 6st 5lbs: she was unplaced. Four months later came that famous first success, on The Chase, in a selling handicap at Haydock, carrying 6st 9lbs; she was not unfancied. Lester Piggott was on his way! By the end of the year he had ridden one winner and two seconds from fourteen rides.

The following year he rode six winners from 120 mounts, but in 1950 he became a genuine 'Boy Wonder'. He won on fifty-two of his 404 mounts, was Champion

The first of 32 Derby rides – at fifteen on the temperamental Zucchero. Note Lester's whip carried until the last moment by the travelling head lad to prevent Zucchero overboiling in the parade. Despite all the precautions Zucchero was left at the start.

Sport & General

Apprentice, and finished eleventh to Sir Gordon Richards in the overall list of winning jockeys – at the age of fourteen!

The season would have wound up even more successfully but for an episode at Newbury on 20 October. Piggott had already earned a reputation for fearless, even reckless riding. He was young, determined, and motivated by a father with a ruthless streak who knew all the tricks of the trade. He had the blind bravado of a driver who has never crashed, a skier who has never broken a leg, a Cresta Rider who has always fallen in the straw. Already he had earned two cautions, and been suspended at Kempton for 'injudicious riding'. The Stewards were watching him, and the older jockeys starting to complain.

'I do like to be beside the seaside. . .?' Lester convalescing at a breezy Brighton in February 1952 from a leg broken in a fall at Lingfield the previous August. In later life preference has been for Nassau or Penang. His companions are owner and professional backer Danny Nossel and father Keith. Topham

Lester was riding a stayer called Barnacle for owner/trainer Arthur Budgett, and took the lead four furlongs out. Scobie Breasley, riding Royal Oak IV, was, as ever, hugging the rails on his inside. Two and a half furlongs out, Barnacle, under pressure, hung over to the rails. Breasley, with a great show, snatched up, stood up in his irons, and then rode like a demon to secure second place. Barnacle had won comfortably, but the wily Breasley objected.

In the Stewards' Room it was no contest. Lester, with his taciturn father, was no match for the wily and experienced Breasley, whose dramatic rhetoric secured the race for Royal Oak IV: Barnacle was placed last.

Worse was to come: Keith Piggott was informed that the matter would be referred to the Stewards of the Jockey Club. The following week, at Newmarket, Piggott senior and junior were marched before the three Stewards. The evidence was heard, and the Stewards announced their verdict. Piggott was to be suspended

'What did I Tulyar?' Cocky Charlie Smirke on the Aga Khan's colt thwarts sixteen-year-old Piggott on Gay Time. Note how far the winner has drifted from the rails under Smirke's left-hand drive. Piggott, until forbidden, was determined to object. Photo Source/Central Press

March 1952 – before the all-weather gallop era. In the '50s and early '60s a make-shift straw canter was the only protection against frost and snow. With the Flat only days away snow still adorned the roofs in the village of Lambourn.
BBC Hulton Picture Library

until the end of the season, still three weeks away. It was the first of many savage punishments that Lester has never accepted were his due. To use one of Lester's favourite expressions, he felt he was 'hard done by'.

In 1951 Barnacle repaid Lester in the Great Metropolitan Handicap at Epsom. It was Lester's first major success on the course that he was to ride better than any man since Steve Donoghue, or perhaps anyone.

Six weeks later he had the first of his thirty-two Derby rides, on the temperamental but brilliant Zucchero. Zucchero was left many, many lengths, but finally jumped off and ran past beaten horses to finish thirteenth of thirty.

'If he'd got off with the others he'd definitely have won,' said Piggott, aged fifteen.

Consolation came in the Eclipse Stakes on the French colt Mystery IX, a horse who never showed comparable form before or after, with Piggott becoming the youngest rider ever to have won the semi-Classic. But again Lester's season ended prematurely. Zucchero was much fancied for the St Leger, but three weeks before the race, on 25 August, Lester broke his leg. Even with three months of the season remaining, Lester had ridden 432 races and won fifty-one.

In 1952, Lester made his first real impact on the Derby. He rode Gay Time to finish second to the Aga Khan's Tulyar ridden by Charlie Smirke. Lester has always believed he should have won the race, but everything went wrong for him.

First, Gay Time pulled off a plate in the paddock, and had to be re-shod. Lester went alone to the start after the other runners and admitted to a feeling of nerves. By the time they reached the start, Gay Time was in a muck sweat, and the race went little better. In a cavalry charge of thirty-three, Gay Time was forced to come wide of his field and lost valuable ground.

Even so, Lester had a winning chance a furlong from home, only for Tulyar, ridden with brilliant cunning by Smirke, to move away from the rails and come close enough to Gay Time to cause him to break his stride. Tulyar won by three parts of a length. As Piggott tried to pull up after the post, Gay Time collided with the rails,

Lester's unforgettable first arrival in the greensward circle at Epsom on Derby Day. The author's father, reporting the event, never forgave Lester his laconic comment: 'It's just another race!' Sport & General

fell over on his head, threw Lester, and galloped off down to Epsom town! It took nearly twenty minutes for Gay Time to return, and for Lester to be able to weigh in.

Lester was determined to object to Smirke, but Gay Time's owner would not hear of it, while the Clerk of the Scales informed him he was too late!

It took Lester two years to obtain revenge. Never Say Die was a little considered 33-1 shot in the Derby of 1954. Lester had hoped for a better ride. In fact his veteran trainer Joe Lawson had tried several other jockeys before Lester received a fateful blue telegram: 'You ride Never Say Die in the Derby'. Lester rode like a veteran, and at eighteen became the youngest winning rider of the Blue Riband. Afterwards, he infuriated an army of Pressmen with his immortal quote, 'It's just another race. . .'.

I have always believed Lester to have been misjudged over this. Knowing Keith Piggott as I do, I suspect that he drummed into Lester, 'Forget it's the Derby – just treat it like any other race.' The advice was locked into Lester's brain! Lester complied with it, and in the following thirty years has continued to do so. No one has ridden Epsom with such amazing, imperturbable sang froid.

On the journey home with his parents Lester was his normal introspective self. By the time they had reached Reading, Lester still hadn't said a word. Finally his mother exclaimed, 'That Never Say Die must be a marvellous horse.' 'Yes, but he's not a patch on Zucchero,' replied Lester, and relapsed into silence.

It was two weeks later that the bottom fell out of Lester's world:

'You are suspended from riding for six months and if you wish to continue to work in stables, you will be apprenticed to a trainer other than your father.' The Duke of Norfolk's face scarcely flickered as he delivered the most damning sentence of Lester's career.

SUSPENSION AND THE MURLESS YEARS

The horses thundered in the short straight at Ascot. In the stands, binoculars were trained upon the Derby winner Never Say Die, and his eighteen-year-old jockey, Lester Piggott.

By then the leaders were battling to hold their position. Lester's cousin, Bill Rickaby, riding Garter, was third, Arabian Knight fourth, and Gordon Richards on Rashleigh, fifth. Piggott, on their heels, made his move on the inside. Almost simultaneously Gordon shook up Rashleigh, whilst Garter was in between the two. What happened next was argued about for months to come, and remains one of the most controversial episodes in post-war racing.

According to Gordon, Lester was completely boxed in, and tried to barge his way out by pushing Garter outwards and on to Rashleigh. 'Lester's horse charged into Garter, and hit my quarters and almost turned me round. Then Never Say Die charged Garter again, and Garter turned me broadside on!' claims Gordon.

According to Lester, however, Gordon saw that he was short of room, and pushed Garter onto *him* to make sure that he couldn't get past the horses in front of him to make his challenge. Those horses were Arabian Knight and Blue Prince II. Then Arabian Knight dived twice to the left, knocking another horse, Tarjoman, onto Rashleigh. But Rashleigh was not to be denied, and went on bravely to win from Tarjoman and Blue Prince II, with Never Say Die fourth.

At first the Stewards objected to Rashleigh, but having heard the evidence of the other jockeys, they turned their attention to Piggott and Never Say Die. Piggott's version that Gordon's mount was to blame cut no ice, and the Stewards suspended Piggott for the remainder of the Royal Meeting, also reporting him to the Stewards of the Jockey Club.

November 1950. Riding out. Keith Piggott's stables were at South Bank, Lambourn, now occupied (and expanded) by Barry Hills. Note the absence of the now-compulsory riding helmets. Sport & General

Two weeks later, Piggott faced the Jockey Club Stewards, headed by the Duke of Norfolk, at Cavendish Square. Those who were determined that the ruthless young upstart should be taught a lesson he wouldn't forget were not to be disappointed. The Stewards announced that they had '. . . taken notice of his dangerous and erratic riding both this season and in previous seasons, and that in spite of continuous warnings he had continued to show complete disregard for the Rules of Racing and the safety of other jockeys.'

His licence was withdrawn, and would not be considered for renewal until he had spent six months in a stable other than that of his father. It was probably the worst moment of Lester's life. Now everything that was most important to him had been taken away. It was certainly a sentence the magnitude of which he couldn't comprehend. No jockey in living memory has received a

Gordon, who rode at no more than 8st 2lbs to the age of fifty. Short and stocky, Gordon, unlike Lester, could use his legs to squeeze, and heels to kick. But 'The Champ' resented the Young Pretender, and ultimately was largely responsible for his temporary downfall. For all that, there remains a colossal mutual respect. Photo Source/Fox

They're off! Gordon, Freddie Fox and Steve Donaghue all fit for the Flat. In the first half of the century the start of the Flat at the windy Carholme on the Monday of Grand National week was second only in importance to the Derby to a Fleet Street Sports Editor. Circulation of newspapers would increase by several hundred thousand copies. The jockeys, relaxed after three weeks winter sports in St Moritz, would travel by train from King's Cross. Nowadays bronzed by the Caribbean sun, they drive by Mercedes to dismal Doncaster – 125 miles, one and three quarter hours from Newmarket.
BBC Hulton Picture Library

Friends and enemies. The rivalry between Piggott and Breasley was the pepper and salt of racing in the late '50s and early '60s. Breasley once said: 'Of all my rivals in Australia or England, Lester was the hardest man to beat.'

Gerry Cranham

The elusive Classic. Lester finally wins the 1,000 Guineas on Humble Duty in 1970 – sixteen years after his first Classic success. Piggott replaced stable jockey Duncan Keith who was unfit owing to weight problems. Colorsport

'There's only one boss here. . . .' The blinkered Juliette Marny shows resentment to restraint as Lester takes her to post for the 1976 Oaks. The Blakeney filly ran out a comfortable four-length winner.

All-Sport/Tony Duffy

Hard, fit and eager to go. The Minstrel takes a strong grip on the way to post for the 1977 Derby.
All-Sport/Tony Duffy

The gamest of the game. The Minstrel answers every call from Lester to fight off Hot Grove (Willie Carson) in a memorable Derby finish. Robert Sangster's colt belied a well-known racing maxim: 'Four white feet – forget him!'
Gerry Cranham

Cousin Bill. In 1954 Bill Rickaby's mother (Lester's aunt), became ward to Lester during his suspension. One of the most popular jockeys of the post-war era, Bill suffered a motor accident in Hong Kong in 1969 from which, tragically, he has never fully recovered. Sport & General

comparable punishment for what amounted to 'trying too hard.'

His resentment was shared between those in authority, and the senior jockeys whom he felt had conspired to bring about his downfall. It was the start of a nightmare of frustration and deprivation, creating a bitter determination to wreak revenge, which I believe has coloured the remainder of Lester's life.

There can be little doubt that the three months between June and September 1954 were the most painful and frustrating of Lester's life. It was decided that Lester should go to the stables of the veteran Newmarket trainer Jack Jarvis, whose owners included several Jockey Club members, notably Lord Rosebery. Lester's cousin, Bill Rickaby, was riding first jockey to the stable at the time.

Lester was boarded with his aunt 'Boie' Lane, wife of the former jockey, Fred Lane. Unhappily the arrangement did not last for long, as Lester's inability to communicate, and his introspective ways, made him an unsatisfactory guest.

So her sister, 'Squif', Bill Rickaby's mother, grasped the nettle, agreeing to put Lester up in return for a minimal rent.

In his autobiography, *First to Finish,* Bill Rickaby recalls the battle of wits that constitutes living with Lester. Bill recounts how his mother once said,

'Do you know, Bill, I think Lester is mending his ways. He bought me a lovely bunch of flowers today.'

Later, Bill's mother rang back feeling slightly less pleased.

'You'll never guess, Lester has taken the cost of the flowers out of his rent!'

On another occasion Lester paid slightly less than his normal weekly rent.

'Why's that? asked his aunt.

'Well,' said Lester, 'You remember the other night I went out? I was in bed for two hours, so it's not fair to pay the full rate!'

Meanwhile, Lester was 'doing his two' (looking after two horses) riding out, and being treated like any other stable lad with Jack Jarvis. Every day he would read the *Sporting Life,* note the horses he would have ridden, and study the results – counting the ten per cent that the Jockey Club, as he saw it, were depriving him of unfairly. He was moody and bitter, and has never accepted that the punishment was of any benefit.

From earning more than £10,000 a year at the age of eighteen – nowadays the equivalent of almost £75,000 – he was back to five pounds a week. Furthermore, he claims to have learnt little or nothing from Jarvis.

'He was never there. He was always ill!'

The establishment believed, however, that good was being achieved in a negative manner. It was felt, rightly or wrongly, that Lester's ruthlessness and determination were attributable to his father's influence. 'Take him away from his father and he'll learn some good habits', they reckoned.

While Lester was 'on remand' two important things happened. Firstly, Sir Gordon Richards, twenty-six times

OPPOSITE PAGE:
Early days. Old-fashioned shoes and trouser bottoms, and archaic telephone. Only the attitude remains the same, thirty years on. Many of Lester's most important winners have been acquired on the 'blower'. One year, at the Jockeys' Dinner, Lester was presented with a mock 'Golden Telephone' by his fellow riders.
Photo Source/Keystone

Champion Jockey, and the finest ambassador that horse racing has ever known, was forced into retirement by a crashing fall at Sandown in July. This meant that Noel Murless, recently moved to Warren Place, Newmarket, and now one of the country's top trainers, was seeking a new stable jockey.

The other important event, which probably led the Jockey Club to believe that 'Piggott had been punished enough' was that Never Say Die won the St Leger. It should have been his ride, but Charlie Smirke stood in for Lester, and the big, long-striding colt won the final Classic by twelve lengths. The first prize was £13,272, ten percent of which would have been Lester's. Two weeks later, on 4 October, the Jockey Club lifted the ban.

Lester had only ten days' notice of his return to the saddle, and during his suspension his weight had risen alarmingly to 9st 7lbs. He ran, starved and sweated to lose the poundage for his first day back, and it was all for the best. On his first day Cardington King won the Isleham Stakes at Newmarket's first October meeting, and the stands shook to the foundations with cheers.

Three wise men (left to right) Lord Rosebery with trainers Jack Jarvis and George Colling. The kindly, but irascible Jarvis, who trained for the Rosebery family for forty-six years, agreed to supervise Piggott's rehabilitation following his suspension in 1954. Sport & General

Lester was back.

Noel Murless, meanwhile, was experiencing surprising difficulty in finding a new stable jockey. Willie Snaith, the dynamic young former Champion Apprentice, who had ridden the brilliant filly Bebe Grande, was approached, but decided to remain loyal to his retainer, Sam Armstrong. The Australian, Scobie Breasley, was also offered the position, but almost unbelievably turned it down because he had just bought a house in Roehampton and felt indisposed to travel two or three mornings a week to ride to work at Newmarket! The Aga Khan suggested, in a letter, that young Manny Mercer would fit the bill, but like Snaith, the stylish Mercer preferred to remain loyal – in his case to George Colling.

Like so many racing matters in the past thirty years, the problem was eventually resolved by a telephone call from Lester Piggott. Murless immediately invited the youthful apprentice – still suspended – to come up to Warren Place to talk. Murless was a determined man, for whom only the best would do. Despite the reservations of one or two of his traditionalist owners, he knew that Piggott was

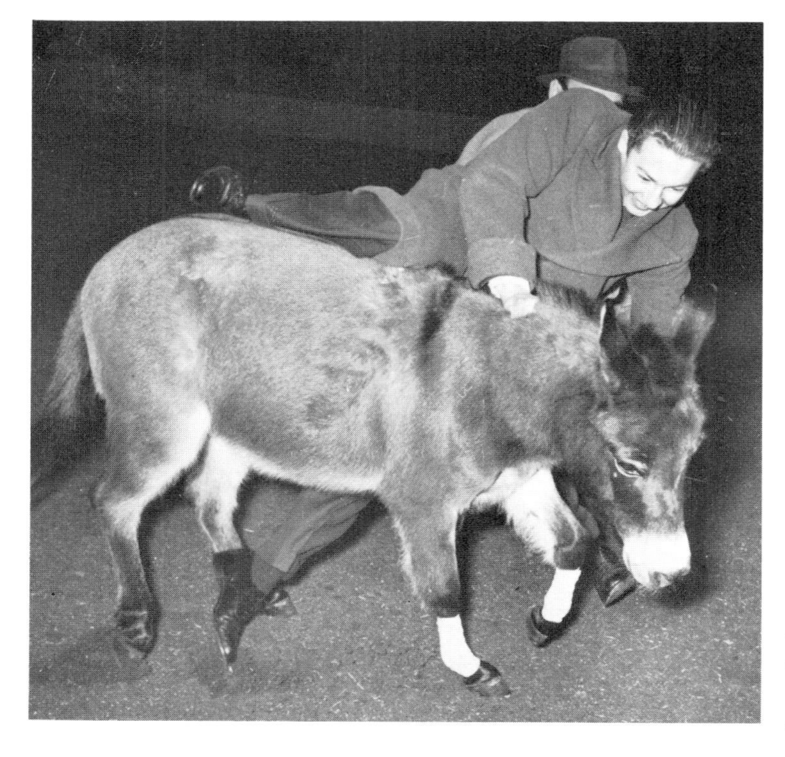

'Lester Who?' Kossmayer's Unrideable Mule is unimpressed by the 'Boy Wonder'. Lester made six attempts to master the mule at Harringay Circus before giving best. Photo Source/Keystone

'Move Over, Grandpa!' Did he really say it? Lester invites Scobie Breasley to give him room. The veteran Aussie, four-times Champion, and Lester's keenest rival for a dozen years, declines.
Gerry Cranham

the man he wanted. A retainer was agreed, and for the first time in weeks Lester returned elated to his digs.

It was a partnership lasting twelve years, that was to carry both men to the pinnacle of their profession. Murless, already leading trainer in 1948, was to become top trainer in four years out of five between 1957-61, and a further four times subsequently. Piggott, the man they said would never become Champion Jockey because of his weight, was to disprove those critics in eight successive years.

More important, with Murless he was to lay the foundations for that record-breaking total of twenty-nine classic wins.

The success of Murless and Piggott was built on a total mutual respect, but Piggott's first impressions were irreverent to say the least.

Lester recalls, 'His hat was one of the oldest I had ever seen. I am sure someone had broken it in for him.'

'As he led his huge string onto the heath, I looked at those enormous feet and I remember feeling pleased that I would never have to ride against him. They looked

like size twenty-sevens! I thought he'd only have to turn them outwards in the stirrups and no one would be able to pass him! It's funny how those first impressions have always stayed with me.'

Lester began the 1955 season with a ruthless determination to make up for lost time, but in this respect Murless was the 'wrong man'. The great trainer was endlessly patient with his horses, and would never allow them to be subjected to a hard race until they were one hundred percent fit.

On outside rides Piggott rode like a demon, and it was in the mid-fifties that he began to attract constant criticism for being too hard on horses. A notable case was the promising two-year-old Final Court, trained by Major Peter Nelson, in the Middle Park Stakes in September 1955. It was generally considered that Piggott had given the colt a thrashing, from which the horse was not to recover. Lester was to ride him once more, in the 1956 2,000 Guineas, where he ran very moderately. Final Court ran his last race in a small field at Newbury later in the year, where he finished almost tailed off.

On a Murless horse such a transgression would not

Crepello justifies universal confidence in a very good Derby. Runner-up Ballymoss went on to win the Irish Derby, St Leger, and the following year's Prix de l'Arc de Triomphe. Crepello never ran again. Note the 'Newmarket boot' on his suspect near fore leg.

Sport & General

Arise Sir Noel! Britain's greatest post-war trainer with wife Gwen and daughter Julie Cecil after his knighthood at Buckingham Palace. It was Murless who harnessed Piggott's youthful exuberance into Classic winning brilliance.
BBC Hulton Picture Library

have been tolerated, and Lester's kindness to Crepello as a two-year-old was well rewarded. Crepello was not only an outstanding horse, but probably represented Murless's finest feat of training. From the first time that he ran as a two-year-old, Murless was concerned by a little notch on his suspensory ligament, and Crepello always wore so-called Newmarket cloths, a type of felt bandage.

Crepello won the 1957 2,000 Guíneas and the Derby with some ease, in the Derby beating Vincent O'Brien's runner Ballymoss, who was later to win the St Leger and Prix de l'Arc de Triomphe.

Sadly, Crepello was not to race again. He was withdrawn – 'amidst controversy' – following a downpour before the King George VI and Queen Elizabeth Stakes at Ascot in July, and he failed to stand training for the St Leger. He was a brilliant horse, and until the O'Brien years certainly the best that Lester had ridden.

Within two days of his second Derby, Lester won his first Oaks – and in the Royal colours.

Both Sir Noel Murless and Sir Gordon Richards – as they are now – agree that Piggott's ride on Carrozza was the finest of his career. Lester squeezed through a gap with two furlongs to run, fought off the Guineas winner Rose Royale II, but up the final hill the Irish filly Silken Glider, ridden by Jimmy Eddery (father of Pat), came with a wet sail.

Lester recalls, 'Carrozza was only tiny, and a bit lazy, but she was as game as a pebble. She was dying in the last

The first Royal Classic. Carrozza, led in by H.M. The Queen following the filly's short head win in the 1957 Oaks. It was The Queen's first Classic winner – and in the view of many, Lester's finest ride.
BBC Hulton Picture Library

hundred yards, but she gave everything she had, and as we passed the post, I didn't know if we'd held on or not.' In fact at the time he was so sure that he had been beaten that he bet the travelling head lad Jim White a 'fiver' that he had not held on. Jim was paid three months later.

It was a week that Piggott and Murless will always remember, not least because Murless had a rare bet, doubling two Classic winners at ante-post odds of 66-1. He also had a further fifty pounds on Carrozza at 100-8 on the day!

The first *great* filly to enter Lester's life was the remarkable grey, Petite Etoile – owned by the Aga Khan – who won the 1,000 Guineas and the Oaks in 1959. Lester rode her with tenderness, sympathy and brilliant judgement. Their success in the 1960 Coronation Cup at Epsom from the previous year's Derby winner, Parthia, was poetry in motion.

St Paddy's Derby. Lester's third and one of the easier ones. Right to Left: Noel Murless, travelling head lad Jim White, and stable lad 'Snuffy' Lawler. To his astonishment, Lawler was given a present of £300 by Lester! Topham

Like so many talented females, Petite Etoile was quirky and unpredictable. She loved to have another grey both in front and behind her in the string; otherwise she sulked. Her first appearance on a racecourse at the now defunct Manchester – on 30 May 1958 – was a complete disaster. She reared up and knocked her lad unconscious, and was then beaten in a two-horse race.

After the race, Lester, with the stable's travelling head lad, Jim White, went round to the ambulance room to see the lad in question, whose name was 'Caffy' Foster.

'Wake up – you alright?' demanded Lester, shaking the lad. Painfully the poor fellow raised himself to his elbow, shook his head and gasped, 'What happened?'

'She got beat,' said Lester. 'Eight lengths.'

'Aagh,' gasped the lad, and fell completely unconscious.

On one occasion Major Cyril Hall, the Aly Khan's Stud Manager, was in Petite Etoile's box, and foolhardily pushing his finger into the filly's neck, boomed, 'You're getting a bit fat old girl!' Petite Etoile grabbed the august gentleman's lapels and lifted him off the ground!

Petite Etoile's most famous defeat – by Aggressor in the King George VI and Queen Elizabeth Stakes – evoked more discussion than any of her wins. What is certain is that Petite Etoile did not truly stay one and a half miles on a searching track. Many thought that Piggott had misjudged the race and given the filly too much to do. Certainly, at one stage she was shut in. On her return, Noel Murless remarked, 'She's only a racehorse – not a machine.'

Recently, an original version of the reason for her defeat appeared in Scobie Breasley's autobiography, *Scobie – A Lifetime In Racing*. Scobie had been nursing a grudge against Lester for some weeks after Lester had 'cut him up', for no reason, according to Scobie, in a race in the Midlands. So Scobie was determined to wreak his revenge on a day when Lester would really suffer.

Scobie relates, 'My mount, the Irish colt Sunny Court, had no real chance of winning, but I decided to do my level best to stop Lester. I didn't intend to break the rules, but was determined to give Lester a hard time, and so square the books. It worked a treat.'

'By the time Lester had shaken me off and got out of the pocket on the rails, Jimmy Lindley and Aggressor had the race won.'

Back to action after yet another suspension. Now twenty-six, note Lester's fashionable turn-ups, and expensive Italian shoes. And who said he's got short arms and long pockets? Photo Source/Fox

Petite Etoile, starting at 5-2 on, was beaten half a length. Typically, Lester said nothing to or about Breasley. Lester could dish it out, but he could take it as well.

These were the vintage Murless years. In 1960, St Paddy won Murless's second and Lester's third Derby, while in the Spring of 1961 there was a colt at Warren Place whom Murless considered the best that he had ever trained. His name was Pinturischio.

I have two vivid recollections of the big horse. One was of watching his work in the morning, which was quite effortless. The second was of meeting casually in the Rutland Arms at Newmarket a close friend of Murless who was responsible for placing a huge stable commission on Sir Victor Sassoon's colt. As the night progressed my friend was increasingly forthcoming about the horse's true ability.

Pinturischio was not to run in the Derby. I remember clearly his final gallop on Racecourse Side on the Saturday before the big day. His work was adequate, and I thought he would probably run in the race. It later emerged that Pinturischio had been doped. What we didn't know until much later was that he was doped *twice*. Alarmed that Pinturischio was in strong work again, the dopers were sent in a second time on the Saturday night after he had done his final work. The following morning he had purged all over his box. With the race just three days away, Murless had no option but to withdraw him.

It is one of racing's open secrets as to who was responsible for Pinturischio's doping. Yet the individual escaped justice, and the firm of bookmakers that he represented continues to thrive.

1960 was also the year of Piggott's first jockey's title. Ten more were to follow from 1964-71, and to underline that Piggott, like good wine, has improved with age, in 1981-82. His total of 188 winners in 1982, at the age of forty-six, was the second largest of his entire career.

Another landmark in 1960 was Lester's marriage to the attractive Susan Armstrong, a union that celebrated its Silver Anniversary on 23 February this year. Predictably, the wedding was a low-key affair in London, with just thirty-eight guests. Lester was twenty-four and his bride, like Lester's mother a former winner of the Newmarket Town Plate, just twenty. A remarkable marriage by any standards, it has survived rocky patches – largely through Susan's loyalty, self-discipline and strength of character.

Lester, for his part, is surprisingly bound by old-fashioned moral standards. When his older daughter Maureen, well into her twenties, gave notice of setting up house with a thoroughly respectable and well-liked young amateur rider, Lester was horrified and quite angry.

A memorable year was climaxed by his success in the Derby and St Leger on St Paddy. One of the most remarkable aspects of St Paddy's success was that Lester gave his lad – who had also looked after Carrozza – a present of £300 in cash – a gift so unaccustomedly

OPPOSITE PAGE. TOP:
The Champion that never was. Pinturischio (Piggott up) winning the Wood Ditton Stakes from Nicodemus. Gambled on to win a fabulous fortune in the Derby, Pinturischio was doped ruthlessly, not once but twice, by bookmaking elements. Press Association

BOTTOM:
The greatest filly: powerful, masculine, quirky, enigmatic, but quite brilliant. Petite Etoile – poetry in motion. She and Piggott brought out the best in each other.
Sport & General

'With all my goods I thee endow. . .?' Lester and Susan married at St Mark's Audley Square in February 1960. A low-key affair, only thirty-eight guests were present.
Photo Source/Keystone

'Well done, Mummy!' Susan Piggott is congratulated by daughter Maureen (aged two and a half) after winning her second Newmarket Town Plate – at that time the only race in which women were allowed to ride against men. Lester's mother, Iris, also twice won the historic event, which was created by Charles II in 1665. Photo Source/Keystone

Deep down he's a big softie! Lester has never spoiled his daughters and encourages Maureen to be independent. But he was deeply hurt when his elder daughter left home to live with a leading amateur rider. Photo Source/Keystone

generous that few people believe the story is actually true!

The Murless years continued without further Classic success. Royal Ascot was invariably the year's highlight, and never to be forgotten was Piggott's bag of eight Ascot winners in 1965. It was probably the worst day for Britain's bookmakers in the past twenty years.

I have always believed that Piggott's success on Casabianca in the Royal Hunt Cup was the strongest ride I have ever seen him give a horse – including Roberto and The Minstrel. Piggott just lifted the big, ungainly grey past four horses in the last fifty yards. No one else, I believe, would have finished in the first three.

It was Piggott's riding of Casabianca in a race at Newbury that evoked the fury of the R.S.P.C.A., who claimed that Piggott had 'soundly thrashed' the grey. Piggott's cruelty was a regular topic of discussion, and occasionally even Lester became aroused by the criticism. On a famous occasion at a party at Newmarket in 1965, Lester came under fierce attack from trainer's wives Pauline Lambton and Serena Oxley. Lester unwisely propelled the contents of his glass into Pauline Lambton's face, whereupon John Oxley, a solid, uncompromising figure, hit Lester firmly on the jaw and knocked him cold!

It was a period in which Lester was becoming restless. Other trainers were winning the Classic races; Ireland's Paddy Prendergast was Champion Trainer three years in a row; the might of Vincent O'Brien's stable was growing to a crescendo.

Lester decided in 1965 that he wished to ride without a formal contract the following year. Murless acceeded, on the basis that Piggott remained stable jockey and was available whenever required.

Something to sing about! Meadow Court, part-owned by the Old Groaner, was a hugely popular winner of the 1965 Irish Sweeps Derby, ridden by Lester. Bing was persuaded to render 'When Irish eyes are smiling' to a delighted unsaddling enclosure.
Sport & General

OPPOSITE PAGE. TOP:
'One man's meat. . . .' Possibly the strongest finish ever ridden by Lester, to win the 1965 Royal Hunt Cup on the grey Casabianca. Lester 'lifted' his reluctant partner past four horses in the last fifty yards. Weepers Boy was second, Zaleucus third and Blazing Scent (far side) fourth. Casabianca's win cost the author a winning bet on the new 'Quadpool' paying £393.10s. for 5/-!
Sport & General

BOTTOM:
Aunt Edith's King George. Lt.-Col. Hornung's mare created a temporary truce between Piggott and Noel Murless after the 'split' in June, 1966. Runner-up was the Irish Derby winner Sodium. Aunt Edith was the second of Lester's seven winners of the King George VI and Queen Elizabeth Diamond Stakes.
Topham

JESUS
NO HOPE
ROYAL HUNT CUP
1 R.MADDOCK
2 G.STARKEY
3 L.PIGGOTT
4 W.WILLIAMSON
5 E.SMITH
6 D.SMITH
7 A.BREASLEY
8 R.HUTCHINSON
G.TURNER
10 J.SIME
11 G.LEWIS
12 D.LETHERBY
J.SHARMAN
15 J.WILSON
16 W.L.THOMAS
17 T.CARTER
18 P.COOK
19 R.READER
A.McGARRITY
21 C.PARKES
22 D.CULLEN
23 D.EAST
W.JESSE
25 D.GREENING
K.STOTT
28 J.HUNTER
RUNNERS

The crumbling relationship came to its crisis in June 1966. Murless had trained a well-bred filly called Varinia, owned by an old friend, Marcus Wickham-Boynton, for the Oaks, and naturally wanted Piggott to ride.

Vincent O'Brien was confident of winning the Classic with Mr Charles Clore's filly, Valoris, ultimately favourite at 11-10. Piggott was determined to ride Valoris – and did so.

It was the end of the road for one of racing's greatest partnerships, although the two masters of their profession came notably together again in July to win the King George with the filly Aunt Edith. Noel Murless, however,was too proud a man to allow his professional requirements to be subject to the whim of a jockey. Piggott's wish was to have his cake *and* eat it, but Murless was determined to acquire a new, top-class stable jockey.

Whatever Piggott has said since, 1967 was *not* the right year to have gone freelance, leaving the Murless stable containing its best horses for years.

'HE'LL NEVER BE CHAMPION'

Over the years Lester has fought battles with owners, trainers, the establishment, the law and occasionally other jockeys. Almost always he has enjoyed the last word. But his longest-running battle, which has continued for over thirty years, has been with his weight. Lester, five feet seven and a half, and the son of a National Hunt jockey, was not constructed in the mould of a Flat Race rider.

Almost all of the great riders world-wide in the past fifty years have been natural 'light-weights'. Sir Gordon Richards rode comfortably at 8 stone till the age of fifty; American Bill Shoemaker, rider of a world record 8,000 plus winners, needs dead weight to ride at 7st 7lbs! Willie Carson and Pat Eddery have no major problems. Only Yves St Martin in France needs to watch the kilos, and occasionally rides at up to 8st 9lbs.

In the fifties, Lester's natural weight was around 10st 7lbs. Part of his aim in riding over hurdles was to contain his weight during the winter months. He only partially succeeded. Lester enjoyed a 'good feed', and in the month following the end of the Flat in early November, his weight would rocket from 8st 5lbs to over 10 stone.

It was widely believed that in the early fifties, during the season, his father encouraged him to take powerful drugs to control his weight. If he did – and there is no evidence to suggest it – it was a system that Lester would soon have realised had only short-term benefits.

On the eve of the 1961 season I remember hearing that Lester had ridden work for the Shrewton trainer Richmond Sturdy in early March, and scaled 10st 7lbs. The next two weeks would be spent sweating, starving, riding and occasionally running, although Lester soon abandoned this practice, on the grounds that it developed weighty leg muscles. (One year, after running most days for three weeks, Lester went to the opening

The Long and the Short of it. Lester and Bill Shoemaker prepare for their match at Ascot in 1982. 'Shoe', so nicknamed because he was incubated in a shoe box after premature birth, won. Scaling less than 7st he has ridden well over 8,000 winners – a world record. Gerry Cranham

The eternal struggle with the scales. This was one ride, at 10 stone, that didn't preclude an egg for breakfast!
BBC Hulton Picture Library

Ouch! Lester without the nowadays favoured goggles, gets mud in the eye riding Tangle over hurdles at Kempton in November 1953. As always, his seat and position of his feet defy the laws of gravity.

Sport & General

meeting at Lincoln and found that he couldn't get his boots on.)

Lester's company in transport has never been agreeable when he has an especially light weight to attempt. At best he would light a malodorous cigar, enveloping his travelling companions with billows of grey smoke. At worst, having slipped into a thick rubber suit, he would close the windows of his Mercedes and put the heater full on, creating the atmosphere of a Turkish Bath. As a means to discourage disagreeable companions from begging a lift, it was devastatingly successful.

Finally, in the early sixties, Lester decided upon a policy of containment. In his own words, he simply 'got out of the habit of eating'.

Even during the winter months he would never relax. Riding commitments during the winter in America,

Cheerful Charlie. Charlie Smirke's frame shows the body's reaction to a relaxation from privation. After half a lifetime in and out of Turkish Baths, Smirke's weight quickly ballooned from 8st 7lbs to 11 stone on retirement. Conversely Doug Smith (left) never had to 'waste' seriously and remains a comfortable eight stone. The other jockey is Australian Edgar Britt.

Sport & General

Hong Kong, Singapore, Australia and South Africa made it easier to maintain self-discipline. It meant abandoning his traditional winter holiday in Nassau, where he would eat copiously and quaff guiltily at his favourite Irish coffee.

His racing diet would be as follows: Breakfast: boiled egg, slice of toast, black coffee (if 'doing light', no egg). Lunch: nothing. Tea: Bar of chocolate. Dinner: Steak or grilled fish. During racing he might drink two small bottles of coca-cola, or half a cup of tea. Racing at Newmarket would mean the indulgence of lunch at home, a thin slice of ham or luncheon meat, and a leaf of lettuce. His liquid intake might be supplemented by a small gin and tonic in the evening.

Kidney problems have always been a jockey's worst enemy, often resulting in kidney stones, a desperately painful calculous formation.

No one in the early sixties, including Lester himself, would have believed that the tall, lean, tortured figure would still be riding in twenty-five years' time.

Lester has genuinely confounded himself. A glance at the files reveals the surprising extent of his durability:

1967 'I'll pack it in in my thirties.'
1969 'I'll ride till I'm forty.'
1971 'I'll ride for another five years.'
1973 'I'm looking forward to another five or six seasons.'

In fact there were another fourteen seasons to come. With each year his desire and capacity to eat became fractionally less.

His approach contrasts sharply with that of most jockeys. They prefer to dine well on Saturday night, putting on up to 6 or 7 lbs, and suffer cruelly in the sauna for three or four hours on Sunday. At the end of their career many, like Charlie Smirke and Harry Carr, see their weight balloon to in excess of 11 stone.

Few British jockeys eat lunch. The French jockeys, with the leading racetracks almost all in the Paris region, are quite the reverse. Many is the time I have seen leading French riders sampling a little Quenelle de Brochet, or Langoustine Mayonnaise, followed by Loup de Mer Au Fenouil, washed down with a glass of white burgundy

LEFT:
Lester at fourteen. The chubby-faced phenomenon had already lost his apprentice allowance and was now obliged to take on Gordon, the Smith brothers and all the rest on level terms. Photo Source/Fox

RIGHT:
Lester at twenty-one. Tall, gaunt, with the weight problems already beginning to bite. At this stage, because of his weight, it was generally agreed that he would never be Champion Jockey.
Provincial Press

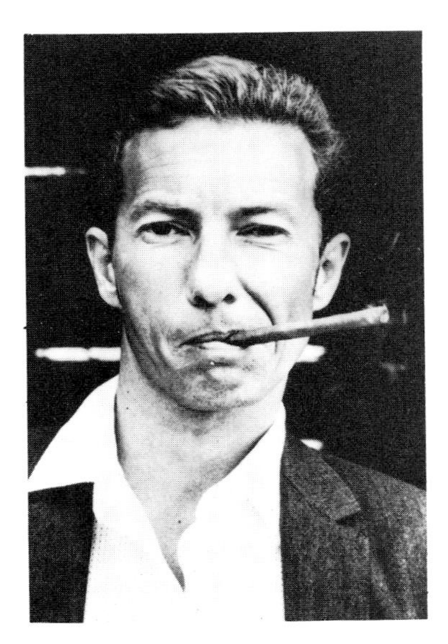

Those damned cigars! L.P.'s effective deterrent to any potential passengers in his Mercedes. This specimen looks good for a full hour and a half of acute discomfort!
Photo Source/Central Press

(although most jockeys prefer claret), before taking a leisurely drive to the Bois de Boulogne.

Unfortunately, certain British riders unused to this indulgence tend to mimic their French counterparts on trips abroad, with disastrous consequences. I well remember a leading British-based rider, having lunched well at Ostend in Belgium, being legged up on a big-race fancy and disappearing promptly over the other side.

Last year in Italy, after an unusually early flight, another British rider installed himself with a friend at a leading hotel and summoned the wine waiter at 9.30 a.m. The following week, despite having ridden in two races that afternoon, the jockey had no recollection of the entire twenty-four hour period!

Lester, however, has never relaxed his self-discipline. A combination of 1,200 cigars a year, a controlled metabolism, and extraordinary strength of mind, have contrived to conquer the problem of indiscreet self-indulgence.

One of the more fascinating aspects of next season's change of profession will be whether or not Lester does alter the eating habits of a lifetime. I have a feeling that Lester's body will be making the rules.

FREELANCE 1967 AND THE O'BRIEN CONNECTION

If there was a turning-point in Lester Piggott's career it was the year 1967.

It was unheard of for a top-class jockey to ride as a freelance. Steve Donoghue was virtually the only man to have tried it, and that was in the autumn of his career.

The racing world was divided between feelings that it was improper, and foolish. Piggott's critics felt that his conduct was motivated by unacceptable greed. They believed his behaviour towards Noel Murless was unpalatable; indeed they felt he should remember his place: a jockey was a jockey and traditionally no more than a stable servant. Others felt that with the talent in Murless's yard in the autumn of 1966 it was quite simply an error of judgement. Piggott believed until the last possible moment that he was going to achieve the best of both worlds.

All the top British jockeys were signed up for the following season. Breasley, Hutchinson, Lewis, Starkey, Mercer and Lindley all had retainers, so it looked as if no one suitable was available. But Lester had reckoned without Murless's capacity to overcome his insular attitude. Acting through the international bloodstock agent George Blackwell, Murless approached the veteran Australian rider, George Moore. After lengthy negotiations, Moore arrived in London on Friday, 14 April 1967. I was the first journalist to greet Moore on his arrival in England – our interview went out live on *Grandstand* on 15 April.

It soon became clear that Moore, now forty-three, was still a rider of exceptional ability. He had ridden in France for the Aly Khan in 1959-60, winning the Prix de l'Arc de Triomphe in 1959 on Saint Crespin III, and the French Derby and Grand Prix de Paris on Charlottesville in 1960. In the same period he had travelled to England to win the 2,000 Guineas, Eclipse and Gold Cup. Unlike

First blood to George Moore. The Australian ace guides Royal Palace to a short head success over Taj Dewan in the 2,000 Guineas. It was a masterpiece of timing and finesse. Lester had suspected that Royal Palace didn't have the 'guts' to be a classic horse. Press Association

most Australians, he adapted immediately to European tracks.

Within five days of arriving in Britain, Moore swept straight into action at the Craven Meeting, winning on Hopeful Venture and Cranberry Sauce on his first two rides.

He and his family moved into an attractive cottage on Newmarket's Eve Stud, but straight away the vibrations were bad. Moore's wife, Iris, felt the premises compared badly with the family's luxurious home in Sydney. To quote an Australian professional punter, 'In Australia a jockey has a social standing somewhere between a brain surgeon and a Supreme Court Judge!' In short, Iris and George were used to celebrity status. The stud cottage did not fit in.

Yet if Moore was irked with personal problems they did not show on the racecourse: his riding was brilliant.

'How's that you Poms?' Australian George Moore on Royal Palace reaping the rewards of Lester's decision to go freelance in 1967. As Mr Jim Joel leads in his first Derby winner, George waves to his wife Iris in the Stands with the message 'mission accomplished'. Lester was on the runner-up, Ribocco.

Sport & General

On 3 May he won the 2,000 Guineas for Noel Murless on Royal Palace by a short head, and the following day the 1,000 Guineas on Fleet.

Lester, meanwhile, having finished 1966 with his largest-ever total of winners, 191, had made his quietest start to a season for many years. His critics gloated over a losing sequence of thirty-one. By the end of May, he was trailing behind Ron Hutchinson in the Jockey's Title.

Royal Palace was a raging favourite for the Derby, and punters were betting heavily on the possibility of Murless and Moore completing a clean sweep in the five Classics. Vincent O'Brien had no Derby horse and Lester was banking on an unpredictable and hitherto-disappointing son of Ribot called Ribocco for his Derby mount.

Lester went through a genuinely bad spell. There was talk of a rift in his marriage and speculation that he was to be named in a divorce case, and at the same time it caused

'Well done, Lester!' Ron Hutchinson congratulates Lester on Ribocco's success in the Irish Sweeps Derby. 'Hutchie' had finished fourth on Gay Garland. Sport & General

him considerable pain to see Moore winning on horse after horse trained by Murless. The final straw came when Royal Palace ran away with the Derby, with Lester on Ribocco second at 22-1.

The turning-point came in the Irish Sweeps Derby. Ribocco, like so many Ribot colts, started to thrive in the summer sun. Royal Palace was not trained for the race, and Murless's runner was a lightly-raced colt called Sucaryl. Ribocco, in the colours of the American platinum millionaire Charles Engelhard, won comfortably by a length from Sucaryl. At least the tide had turned for racing's most famous freelance.

Although Piggott was having the occasional ride for Murless, the relationship reached crisis point in the Eclipse Stakes. George Moore chose to ride the classic filly Fleet, in preference to the progressive four-year-old Busted, who was ridden by Bill Rickaby. Piggott was on Jolly Jet. According to George Moore, early in the straight Fleet received a painful blow in the face from Piggott's whip, and curled up. Busted went on to win the race at odds of 8-1.

'That little so-and-so will never ride for us again,' stormed Gwen Murless. Noel was not disagreeing.

Racing's own 'Goldfinger'. In fact Charles W. Engelhard was the Platinum King, who moved into European racing in a big way. Nijinsky's Derby gave him a special 'buzz'. He celebrated, as always, in Coca Cola. Sport & General

The turning point. Ribocco beats Sucaryl (George Moore) in the Irish Sweeps Derby to give Lester his first Classic success after turning freelance. From August onwards the Moore magic began to wane.

Topham

Three weeks later, Moore won the King George VI and Queen Elizabeth Stakes on Busted to round off a fabulous summer.

But in August there were rumblings of discontent. During the summer, Iris Moore had pursuaded her husband to lease a luxury flat in Cadogan Square, just five minutes' walk from Harrods. George continued to use the Eve Stud cottage for gallop mornings and Newmarket races. There was talk of strange telephone calls to Moore during the night. One evening all of Iris's dresses in the London flat were found shredded to pieces.

By September there were strong rumours that Moore would not return to England in 1968. Tales of reprisals by Australian punters when Moore's successful run came to an end and the wrong horses started to win, were rife.

Finally, Moore went missing for forty-eight hours: he simply vanished. I was sent on a wild goose-chase to Chantilly for BBC Sportsnight to try and locate him. In the end he turned up in the Hotel Maurice, in Paris's expensive Rue Royale. The mystery deepened.

Moore then informed Murless that for personal reasons he was returning to Australia and not coming back in 1968. His last day's riding was at Newmarket on 21 October. Royal Palace had met with a set-back in his preparation for the St Leger and missed the final Classic, but now Murless had readied the Derby winner for the Champion Stakes, which was to be Moore's last ride for Murless.

The sleek Ribocco beautifully nursed by Lester, wins his second Classic, the St Leger. The Ribot colt was a length and a half too good for The Queen's Hopeful Venture (George Moore).
Sport & General

It was a strange day. I arranged to meet Moore at 1.30 for an interview on BBC TV, but for the first time in our relationship he let me down, and didn't appear. In the Champion Stakes market there was opposition to Royal Palace, although he started at 11-8 on. In the race he ran far below his true form, and finished only third behind Reform and Taj Dewan. Sir Noel Murless has always believed he was capable of running a better race than he did. So Moore, the shooting star, flew back to the other side of the world, and Lester allowed himself a wry smile.

Whether Lester believed that Murless would now reinstate him on a freelance basis, history does not relate. If he did believe it Lester was to be disappointed. Murless, encouraged by his Scots-born wife, engaged the brilliant Ayrshire apprentice Sandy Barclay to be first jockey at Warren Place in 1968.

By the end of the year honours were almost even. Murless was Champion Trainer with record earnings of £256,899. Piggott remained Champion Jockey, but with only 117 winners – seventy-four fewer than the previous year.

However, Ribocco had won the St Leger, and in addition the autumn two-year-old races had thrown up two brilliant young horses in Sir Ivor and Petingo. Lester had both very firmly in his sights, and within his grasp.

1968 was the coronation of the next great partnership in racing, that between Piggott and Vincent O'Brien. It was a relationship, fuelled subsequently by the financial input of Mr Robert Sangster, that was to bring both men untold wealth, and ultimately raise them to multi-millionaire status. Vincent O'Brien, who trains at Ballydoyle, Cashel, Co. Tipperary, is generally considered the greatest post-war trainer. He started in the forties and fifties with National Hunt horses, and won three successive Cheltenham Gold Cups and three successive Grand Nationals, an unprecedented and unrepeated feat.

He then switched to training flat racehorses with considerable success, and has now won six Derbys.

His link-up with Robert Sangster began in the mid seventies. Sangster had owned racehorses in Great Britain for a number of years with middling success, but with O'Brien formed a syndicate that enabled them to bid for the finest American-bred yearlings in Kentucky.

The Minstrel was their first major success, and for the past ten years they have dominated European racing and breeding, attracting into the market such high rollers as Stavros Niarchos and the Dubai Royal Family.

Ten years ago it was unthinkable for a yearling to fetch one million dollars in the ring. Now the record is in excess of ten million dollars. Sir Ivor, Nijinsky, Roberto, The Minstrel and Alleged now have a collective value of well over a hundred million dollars. Off-shore companies either owned, or part-owned, by Lester, have a share in or breeding rights to most of these stallions.

When the dust settles Lester will probably admit that Sir Ivor was his favourite good horse. Of all his great big-race rides, nothing was more spectacular than his thrilling Derby win on Sir Ivor on 29 May, 1968.

Sir Ivor won three races as a two-year-old, the last of them the valuable Grand Criterium at Longchamp. Lester set him a fair task in the straight, but when he set him alight, the reaction was explosive.

'He quickened so fast he almost ran out from under me,' Lester grinned.

23

OPPOSITE PAGE:
The Minstrel moves sweetly to post on Derby Day. After his defeat in the Irish 2,000 Guineas, which disappointed Vincent O'Brien, Lester told Vincent: 'If you run him at Epsom, I'll ride him.' Vincent ran him. . . . Gerry Cranham

The A-Team: owner Robert Sangster, trainer Vincent O'Brien and Lester dominated the 1977 European season, together winning the Derby, Irish Sweeps Derby, King George VI & Queen Elizabeth Stakes, Prix de l'Arc de Triomphe and many others. All three men are millionaires several times over.
Gerry Cranham

The memorable climax to a famous year. Alleged wins his first and only Lester's second Prix de l'Arc de Triomphe from the British-trained but New Zealand bred Balmerino (Ron Hutchinson).

OPPOSITE PAGE:
Amid pre-race controversy, Lester replaced Wally Swinburn at the eleventh hour on Blue Wind to win his fifth and easiest Oaks.
Gerry Cranham

Moorestyle sets off on the tan gallop on Newmarket Heath. Lester liked to 'breeze' the champion sprinter whenever possible coming up for a race. Gerry Cranham

2

4

2

On the eve of Sir Ivor. Lester and master trainer Vincent O'Brien relaxed and confident on Epsom Down at 8.00 a.m. Thirty-three hours later Vincent's nerves were put to a stern test.
BBC Hulton Picture Library

After Sir Ivor's first win, his owner, the American ambassador to Ireland, Mr Raymond Guest, stuck a bet of £500 each way on Sir Ivor at 100-1 with William Hill to win the following year's Derby.

Vincent O'Brien experimented by sending Sir Ivor to the mild Mediterranean climate of Pisa for the winter. It was an enterprise that almost back-fired. Sir Ivor developed an abcess in his foot, which caused his leg to swell like a balloon. After three weeks' inactivity Sir Ivor was exuberantly fresh and one morning got loose and almost fell into a huge dyke!

The weather was very wet in the spring of 1968, and the ground was heavy when Sir Ivor won the Ascot 2,000 Guineas Trial. Vincent O'Brien decided to send him to Newmarket to complete his preparation on the invariably perfect ground of the famous heath. I filmed Sir Ivor working on Racecourse Side two days before the 2,000 Guineas and he looked magnificent – a machine.

Four days earlier we had filmed a superb tracking shot of Petingo working on Railway Land. Petingo's elastic

OPPOSITE PAGE. TOP:
Saint-Martin's revenge. France's finest post-war jockey, for whom Lester has both affection and respect, wins one of the most exciting races for the 'Arc' in living memory on Akiyda from Lester on Ardross. It was an A-day. The result 1. Akiyda, 2. Ardross, 3. Awaasif, 4. April Run.
Gerry Cranham

BOTTOM:
Ardross came home alone to win his second Gold Cup. At the age of six he was better than ever. He remains one of Lester's favourite horses. Ed Byrne

4

The world is my oyster! Lester admires the Washington D.C. International Trophy with owner Raymond Guest (centre) and Vincent O'Brien. This was one victory on home ground that the winning owner enjoyed to the full. Topham

stride made it some of the best racing film I have ever witnessed.

Lester had chosen to ride Sir Ivor, and Joe Mercer was booked for Petingo. It was a magnificent 2,000 Guineas, and Sir Ivor, backed down to 11-8, was a brilliant winner. Lester held up the big colt at the rear, made his move going into The Dip, and went away to win by one and a half lengths. Ladbrokes' representative, reflecting an element of opinion that Sir Ivor would not stay one and a half miles, on account of his pedigree, was foolhardy enough to offer 4-1 about Sir Ivor for the Derby.

I still possess my ante-post voucher. I have never been more certain that a horse would win the Derby. Vincent brought Sir Ivor to Epsom on the Monday of Derby week and allowed me to film him on Tuesday morning at 7.15 a.m. Again, he looked magnificent. Lester was predictably monosyllabic, but confident. It was up to him to ensure that Sir Ivor lasted the trip.

Raymond Guest had an official engagement in Ireland at the unveiling of the Kennedy Memorial, and so was compelled to watch the Derby on TV. Poor Raymond must have had heart failure. Lester waited and waited and waited. At the distance (240 yards from the finish) Connaught and Sandy Barclay had gone three lengths clear. At last Lester made his move, and with brilliant

OPPOSITE PAGE. TOP:
A famous 2,000 Guineas. The great Sir Ivor, Piggott up, pulverizes Petingo (Joe Mercer). It was Petingo's first defeat. Lester could have ridden either horse, but predictably chose correctly. Sport & General

BOTTOM:
Sir Ivor's sensational burst of speed to win the Derby going away by a length and a half from Connaught. So certain was eighteen-year-old Sandy Barclay of success on the runner-up a furlong from home that he burst into tears after the race. Sport & General

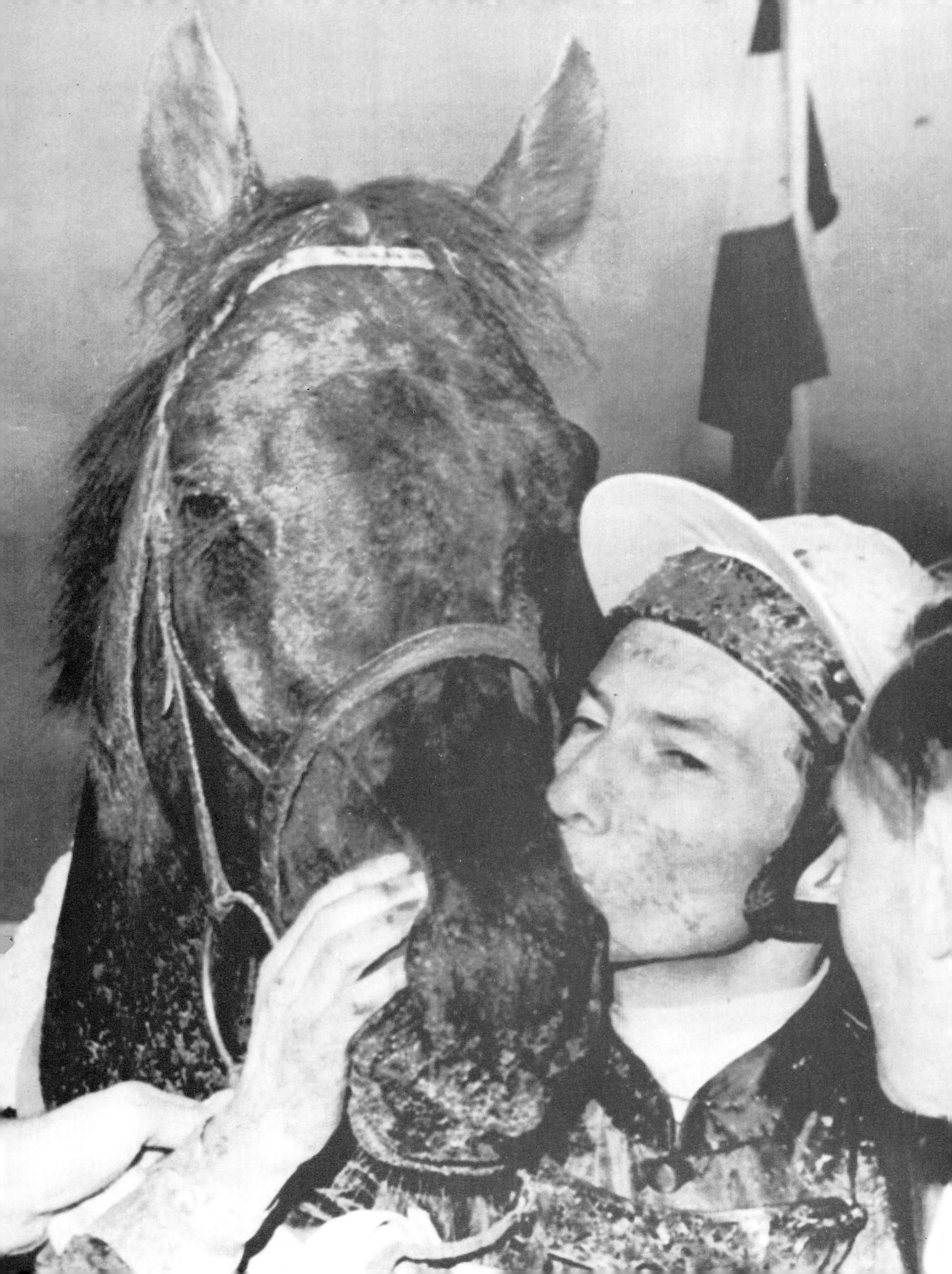

acceleration Sir Ivor made up three lengths in a hundred yards, struck the front fifty yards from home, and won going away by one and a half lengths. It was the most devastating finishing thrust that anyone could remember in the Derby.

That evening I visited a friend who had viewed the race through a haze of marijuana. She told me it was the biggest 'turn-on' she had ever experienced!

Sir Ivor failed in the Irish Sweeps Derby, unable to stay the Curragh's severe mile and a half (ridden by Liam Ward, Vincent O'Brien's retained jockey in Ireland). He also failed in the Eclipse, and the Prix de l'Arc de Triomphe. But, bravely campaigned, he was magnificent in the Champion Stakes, and finally gained a memorable win in the Washington D.C. International. It was after this race that the American Press, not understanding Sir Ivor's problems and the European race riding technique, wrote, 'Piggott rode like a bum'!

Lester laughed his way to the bank; and returned twelve months later to win again on Karabas. Faced by some red-faced scribes, by now aware that they had underrated the man, Lester enjoyed himself.

'When did you think you were going to win the race?' asked a local scribbler. 'About two weeks ago,' replied Lester, and turned tail.

It was remarkable that within two years Vincent O'Brien should produce another Champion, at his best perhaps superior to Sir Ivor. But that was the level of Nijinsky. His marvellous career continued for eleven races – the Dewhurst Stakes, the 2,000 Guineas, the Derby, Irish Sweeps Derby, the King George and the St Leger – before his first defeat in the Prix de l'Arc de Triomphe.

In the 2,000 Guineas, at 7-4 on, he was the shortest-priced favourite since Colombo in 1934. On the day he didn't impress everyone – and particularly those who watch only the end of a race. The reason was simple. Lester's orders were not to take any chances. Accordingly, in a fast-run race, Lester lay far handier than he would otherwise have done. Such was his speed that he could have picked off the flying French colt Amber Rama at any time.

OPPOSITE PAGE:
'I didn't know you cared!' Lester obliges the American photographers with a most un-Piggott-like gesture after Sir Ivor's dramatic win in the Washington D.C. International.
Topham

The majestic Nijinsky. Lester steers the great horse to his tenth straight – and most impressive – win in the King George VI & Queen Elizabeth Stakes. The previous year's Derby winner Blakeney is in vain pursuit. Sport & General

When Lester went to win his race, Nijinsky did not produce the acceleration he would have done if Lester had been allowed to lie further off the pace. Also, when he hit the front, Nijinsky started to idle.

Nonetheless, he won nicely by two and a half lengths – and William Hill made the mistake of offering 5-2 against Nijinsky for the Derby, on 3 June, 1970.

Nijinsky's year was one of the best quality Derbys I have seen.

Bill Williamson rode the great, long-striding, white-blazed French colt, Gyr, whose trainer, the legendary Etienne Pollet, had remained in harness purely to train Gyr as a three-year-old. Neither Pollet nor Williamson believed that he could be beaten. I was hugely impressed by the success of Mr Gerald Oldham's colt Stintino in the Prix de Guiche at Longchamp on 19 April – the same day as Gyr won the Prix Daru.

The strength of the opposition, combined with the usual stamina-doubts over American-bred horses, led to Nijinsky starting odds against in the Derby for the first time in his entire career.

It was another memorable race. Piggott rode the classic waiting race, conserving his mount's stamina, but remaining within striking distance. The outsider, Great Wall, at 66-1, ran the race of his life till Bill Williamson made his move with two furlongs to go. Stintino came with a flourish on the wide outside. At the distance, Piggott produced Nijinsky with a flourish between horses. There was a short sharp tussle before Nijinsky drew away in style by two and a half lengths, in the fastest time since the record-breaking Mahmoud in 1935. Bill Williamson couldn't believe there was a horse in training that could treat Gyr in such a way. Gyr duly went on to win the Grand Prix de St Cloud with ease.

Nijinsky continued on his victorious way. His effortless, hard-held win in Ascot's King George VI and Queen Elizabeth Stakes was the most impressive of his career. But within a week of his return to Ireland, misfortune struck. He was beset with a particularly virulent form of ringworm, which caused a great deal of his skin to become raw. He could not be ridden, and O'Brien would have favoured giving him a prolonged rest.

Unhappily, as it transpired, the colt's owner, Charles Engelhard, expressed a desire that Nijinsky should be trained for the St Leger on 12 September. No horse had won the famous Triple Crown since Bahram in 1935. In principle it looked like a formality for Nijinsky.

Vincent O'Brien's autumn objective for Nijinsky was the Prix de l'Arc de Triomphe on 4 October. To run in the St Leger created two disadvantages: firstly, a rushed preparation following the unpleasant skin disease, and secondly, a race over a distance two and a half furlongs further than the Arc, and almost certainly beyond Nijinsky's best. Nonetheless, O'Brien complied with his owner's wishes, and Nijinsky went to Doncaster at odds of 7-2 on.

His rivals were determined to test his stamina, and the race was run at a fierce pace, Piggott cruised into the lead a furlong and a half from home to win easing up. No one truly knew how much Lester had in hand, but I have always believed that the ace poker player was mighty relieved that no one had asked to see his hand. The winning margin was only one length – and in my eyes Nijinsky's tank was empty. Nijinsky lost 31lbs weight in the St Leger, by far the greatest loss he had sustained during his career. O'Brien had three weeks in which to restore Nijinsky to his peak. His coat was improving every day, and Nijinsky was working well.

The 1970 Arc was without doubt one of the two most controversial races that Lester has ever ridden. Today, fifteen years after the event, the legendary O'Brien still

Nininsky's St Leger win made him the first Triple Crown winner since 1935. For Lester it was his fifth of eight St Legers, for Nijinsky his 11th straight win, but sadly also his last.
Gerry Cranham

TOP:
Nijinsky's St Leger. Lester was able to relax the great horse despite his clearly visible pre-race tension. Here he is sandwiched between Melody Rock (Bill Williamson) (far side) and the eventual third, Politico (Sandy Barclay). Gerry Cranham

BOTTOM:
The awful reality of defeat. Even before the race Nijinsky had boiled over. Now Lester returns drained of colour and shattered. The unbeatable was beaten. Only the lady with the handbag doesn't realise.
Rex Features

blames Piggott for his colt's defeat. In my view, having watched the race dozens of times, seldom, if ever, has Lester been so unfairly criticised. O'Brien has stated that he asked Lester to lie up close to the leaders and not give his mount too much ground to make up in the straight. Lester, for his part, knew the course, the opposition, and above all, Nijinsky's capabilities.

He told Vincent, 'I don't care if there are a hundred horses in front of me.'

Partly because of Nijinsky's reputation there was an unusually small field for the Arc – only fifteen runners. But the pace was strong – there were two pacemakers – and Lester was determined to give Nijinsky every chance to last the trip.

He settled Nijinsky four from the rear, but close enough to the good horses. When the field swung into the straight, Lester, anxious to take no chances following the digestion of the copious written instructions from O'Brien, pulled towards the outer. An opening did not immediately appear, and Lester had to switch twice, very quickly, before he saw clear daylight. But he was no more than six lengths from the leader.

The old Nijinsky would have won with ease from that position. For a few seconds he looked – and felt – like the old Nijinsky. A hundred yards from the finish he drew upsides the outsider Sassafras, ridden by the great St Martin.

The race was won. But no! he had headed Sassafras, but he wasn't drawing away. Piggott was anxious. *He went for his whip.* Still he couldn't shake off Sassafras. And then, in the last two strides, *disbelief,* he was beaten! Sassafras, at 18-1, had won by a head. Thousands of racegoers at Longchamp, and millions watching on TV, were quite simply stunned.

Lester had never won the Arc, and this was the ultimate disappointment. Within minutes, pundits, punters peaking through their pockets, and individuals close to the horse who should have known better, were pointing the finger at Lester.

Even today, O'Brien is convinced it was Piggott and not Nijinsky who lost the Arc. But a look at the head-on camera patrol shows quite clearly why he lost. When

Piggott, in desperation, hit Nijinsky, the horse flinched and swerved left. It was the first time since the Derby that he had felt the whip. Whether he was tired through not being at his best, or whether what happened reflected a weakness, he lost the race through his reaction to that smack with the whip.

Nijinsky, the unbeaten Triple Crown winner – the 'Horse of the Century' – had been beaten, and Lester had to carry the can. I was one of the few that refused to condemn Lester. Bitter arguments raged, and hostilities built up which in some cases have never been mended. It looked like an argument that would long continue, but never be resolved.

Then Vincent O'Brien made the fateful decision that he will surely rue until the end of his life. Nijinsky was to run in the Champion Stakes just thirteen days after the Arc. O'Brien is probably the greatest all-round practitioner of training skills that any of us will ever see, but with Nijinsky he suffered an inexplicable blind spot. Despite constant examination of the Arc film, he would not accept that Nijinsky had displayed a weakness.

Nijinsky had lost his unbeaten record so there was nothing to lose. Let him, felt Vincent, go out in a blaze of glory. So Nijinsky went to Newmarket, and the worst happened. The evil spirit that showed its head at Longchamp had burgeoned into a fully-grown monster. Nijinsky boiled over, reared up, and was actually trembling during the parade, and at the start he fell to pieces.

In the race, Lorenzaccio, owned by Charles St George and trained by Noel Murless, made all the running. Nijinsky at 11-4 on was beaten one and a half lengths. Once again he had found nothing under the whip. It was a sad end to a marvellous career, and a sad day for anyone who loves horses. No true enthusiast likes to see a good horse beaten.

Lester, in his usual manner, had kept his thoughts private throughout the post-Arc agonising, but later he reflected, 'Nijinsky was a brilliant racehorse, of course, but he was highly strung. He always seemed to be looking at birds. He hadn't Sir Ivor's character.'

O'Brien, asked to compare Nijinsky with his other great horses, stated recently, 'I would have to rate him first or second, him or Sir Ivor. For brilliance, Nijinsky. For toughness, Sir Ivor.'

It was a bitter end to an otherwise wonderful season for Lester: four Classics (including his first 1,000 Guineas on Humble Duty); the Jockeys' Title for the seventh successive year; countless big-race wins all over Europe. But Lester was tired and his health went through a bad spell.

One autumn evening, thinking about Nijinsky, his mind went back to a conversation with his father years before. With successes in England, France, Ireland and further afield, Lester worked out, 'I've ridden 200 winners this year.' 'What about the ones you didn't win on?' replied his father.

THE SEVENTIES – A CHANGE OF PACE

After the year of Nijinsky, anti-climax was almost inevitable. In 1971, Lester was again Champion Jockey, his total of 162 winners being identical to the previous season. But Vincent O'Brien had not produced a Classic three-year-old, and his best two-year-old, Roberto, had been a disappointment in the Grand Criterium.

It seemed as if Lester's hopes of 1972 were centred around Newmarket's 'talking horse', Crowned Prince, (trained by Bernard van Cutsem), an own brother to the Kentucky Derby winner Majestic Prince, and who cost a world record at the time – $510,000 as a yearling. In the Dewhurst Stakes, with Piggott up, he had beaten Rheingold by five lengths, and went into winter quarters a clear favourite for the Derby.

By November 1971, Lester had committed himself to ride Crowned Prince the following season. He had also resolved to 'wind down' in 1972.

'I don't think I'll ride quite as much as I have been doing, because I don't really want to go and ride night and day at all the little meetings.

'If anyone can take the title from me they'll take it. There are two boys having a lot more rides than me, Tony Murray and Willie Carson, and they've got to be hard to beat – they're having up to 200 more rides than me! It's the law of averages that they're going to beat me sometime!'

Lester was as good as his word. From 162 winners, his total dropped to 103 and Willie Carson, with 132 wins, became Champion Jockey for the first time. Lester – and others – genuinely believed that, at thirty-six, he was entering the autumn of his career.

Vincent O'Brien, meanwhile, was resigned to Lester's riding Crowned Prince in the Classics, so determined to obtain the services of the next best man. Accordingly, a retainer was arranged with that superb big-race rider Bill

OPPOSITE PAGE:
The powerful record-priced Crowned Prince with half-cup blinkers and Australian nose-band, proving a real handful. Lester agreed to ride him in the 1972 Classics, but by April he had been retired from racing. Sport & General

OPPOSITE PAGE. TOP:
Cajun wins the Greenham Stakes from Tender King (nearside) and Macmillion. Unhappily, the chestnut had to be withdrawn from the 2,000 Guineas on the day of the race because of a bruised foot Ed Byrne

BOTTOM:
Critique, in the colours of Garo Vanian (brother of Souren), responds to a touch of Piggott genius to win Royal Ascot's Hardwicke Stakes. After he had lost his form as a three-year-old, Piggott and Henry Cecil achieved a metamorphosis in this temperamental horse. Ed Byrne

Williamson, who was contracted to ride Roberto in all his races.

'Weary Willie', the likeable if taciturn Australian who had chased home Robero on Gyr, had established his 'big-race' reputation with masterful Arc de Triomphe victories on Vaguely Noble (1968) and Levmoss (1969). On each occasion Lester had finished runner-up, on Sir Ivor and Park Top.

The new seaon started with a major set-back. Crowned Prince was 9-4 on favourite for the Craven Stakes, but ran a disastrous race and finished fourth of five. Almost everyone in Newmarket knew that Crowned Prince had 'gone in the wind' – everyone, that is, except Lester. 'He's closer to the horse than anyone, but he's so bloody deaf he's the only one who can't hear,' exclaimed one wag.

Before long a soft palate was diagnosed, and Crowned Prince retired. Lester was without a Classic mount. Lester climbed onto an ordinary horse called Grey Mirage, who had won two Classic trials, in the 2,000 Guineas.

High Top, a stable companion to Crowned Prince, but the mount of Willie Carson, was 85-40 favourite, with Roberto second best in the market at 7-2. It was a vile day, and Carson rode High Top straight down the centre of the course, made all the running and beat Roberto by half a length. Grey Mirage was unplaced. Roberto had run a good race, but there was a feeling in the O'Brien camp that Williamson had given the horse too much to do. There was, in fact, a lack of confidence in the forty-nine year-old Australian. It was fuelled by Piggott approaching O'Brien after the race and saying, 'If I'd ridden him, he'd have won. You'd better let me ride him at Epsom.'

In the following fortnight Lester's name was associated with half a dozen different horses. Finally, to many people's surprise, Lester homed in upon Ballydoyle. Roberto, of course, was presumably not available, but Lester appeared to show interest in a horse called Manitoulin, who had gained a surprise win in the Royal Whip at The Curragh, and who eventually started at 66-1 for the Derby.

Lester flew over to ride Manitoulin in a gallop with Roberto. According to O'Brien, as quoted in *Vincent*

4

Diesis displays his terrific stride on the way to post for the Middle Park Stakes. The own brother to Kris later became the first horse to complete the Middle Park/Dewhurst Stakes double for seventy-three years. Sadly, Diesis failed to train on as a three-year-old. Ed Byrne

O'Brien's Great Horses by Ivor Herbert, 'Roberto was a lazy horse. He'd pull himself up as soon as he passed a horse. Lester watched Roberto do that when he passed him in the gallop and said, "That horse won't win at Epsom!"'

But after the gallop Lester went over to Vincent and asked him about Roberto. 'I told him that was how he always worked,' recalls Vincent.

Now fate was to take an unexpected hand. At Kempton on 27 May, with the Derby just eleven days away, Williamson, riding a horse called The Broker, took a crashing fall and injured a shoulder.

Vincent O'Brien now came under pressure from two sides – from Lester, reinforcing his claims to be the best man for the job, and undertaking to keep himself available, and from Roberto's owner, the American John Galbreath, owner of the Pittsburg Pirates, and a self-professed expert on athletes' injuries. Williamson, meanwhile, was undergoing treatment from the expert

'Weary Willie', the modest, reserved Australian, described by Lester as the best big-race jockey in the world. Williamson retired the season following the Roberto debacle and died not long afterwards from cancer. It could have been from a broken heart.
Photo Source/Central Press

OPPOSITE PAGE. TOP:
A thrilling finish to the Yorkshire Oaks. Awaasif (Piggott) gets up to beat Willie Carson on Swiftfoot (part-hidden) with Dish Dash (Bruce Raymond) finishing fast on the stands side. Note the similarity in style between Piggott and Raymond, although Piggott is riding on a fractionally longer reign than usual. Ed Byrne

BOTTOM:
Glorious Goodwood, Chalon (Piggott) stretches away from Wink (Willie Carson) against the lovely back-drop of the Sussex Downs. In Lester's hands she went from strength to strength. This was her seventh successive win. Ed Byrne

'Steve'. Son of an Irish-born Warrington steel-worker Donaghue was the greatest Derby jockey this century before Piggott. Like Piggott, he had scant respect for conventional loyalties and stable retainers, but his charm and generosity carried him through all crises.

Photo Source/Keystone

physiotherapist Bill Tucker, and eventually assured O'Brien that he would be fit to ride. Bill Tucker had given him the 'OK', and Williamson took a couple of rides at Salisbury on Tuesday, the eve of the Derby, to prove himself race fit.

Unknown to him, Galbreath and O'Brien had already made their decision to replace him. Williamson was summoned to meet the owner and trainer at Claridges in London on the Monday. According to O'Brien, who does not shirk responsibility for the decision, Galbreath and

Williamson were already there when he arrived at the meeting. Galbreath had told the jockey that he had considerable knowledge of athletes' injuries, and that Williamson could not possibly be fit to ride. Piggott was to ride his horse, but Williamson could receive the same present as Piggott if the horse won. Williamson was shattered, and disbelieving. He was a man with the highest reputation for honesty and integrity, and he felt that this had been called into question.

At 7.15 on the Tuesday morning it was Piggott who rode Roberto at exercise on the course, while a sad Williamson motored to Salisbury to ride Mishmumpkin in the first race. Mishmumpkin finished unplaced, but Williamson confirmed himself one hundred percent fit for Epsom.

The racing public was savagely divided. There were those who cried, 'Good old Lester', believing that the world's greatest jockey was beyond reproach. Besides, he was English . . . . There were others who considered the episode to be nothing short of a scandal – a cynical, unethical breach of a clear Gentlemen's Agreement; an action to drag the Sport of Kings into the gutter.

It was an unusually dramatic prelude to the Derby. The race itself achieved a level of drama unparalleled in post-war years. For the first time ever, there were boos as well as cheers as Piggott cantered to the post. But the public made Roberto a clear favourite at 3-1. Noel Murless's runner, Yaroslav, and the French challenger Lyphard, were joint second favourites at 4-1.

In the straight there were only three horses with a winning chance. Lyphard had run half across the course at Tattenham Corner, while Yaroslav, after resenting the stalls, never showed. The outsider Rheingold took the lead from Pentland Firth a furlong from home, as Roberto challenged between the two.

The battle to the post was epic. For a few strides, Rheingold, ridden by the light-weight Ernie Johnson, looked stronger. But Rheingold began to edge left down the infamous Epsom camber. The horses were locked together. Ernie Johnson, his whip in his left hand, didn't dare move his hands from the reins. Piggott, perched high on his horse's withers, brought down his whip seven

'He's tough as nails, Ma'am.' Lester discusses The Minstrel with H.M. The Queen after his win in the 'King George'. The Minstrel was retired to stud in America with a valuation of $9 million. The following year The Queen sent her mare Joking Apart to The Minstrel and bred the filly Sans Blague, a good winner.
Sport & General

times in the last fifty yards of the race. Photo finish! But the drama did not end there. A Stewards' Enquiry, the first in the history of the Derby, was called.

Alone in the stands stood Bill Williamson, balancing the prospect of ten percent of £63,735 with the thought that he had almost certainly lost his last winning chance in the Epsom Derby. 'Here is the result of the photo finish on the Derby: First, Number Nineteen, Roberto . . . .' The rest of the announcement was drowned, Piggott had won his sixth Derby, equalling the record of Jem Robinson and Steve Donoghue

But the Stewards' Enquiry was still to come. Had Roberto edged away from the rails? Was it Piggott's fault that Johnson couldn't use his whip? The result of the Enquiry was that the placings were to remain unaltered.

However, the play was not over. In the following race Bill Williamson cantered to post amidst sympathetic cheering on the 5-1 shot, Captive Dream. A few minutes later the cheers were in a different key. Williamson had won the Woodcote Stakes by two and a half lengths, with Piggott riding the favourite only third. In the last race, Williamson completed a 47-1 double on Capstrano, his only other ride. Honours, to all intents, were even.

For Williamson there were better things to come. In the Irish Sweeps Derby on 1 July, he landed the £58,905

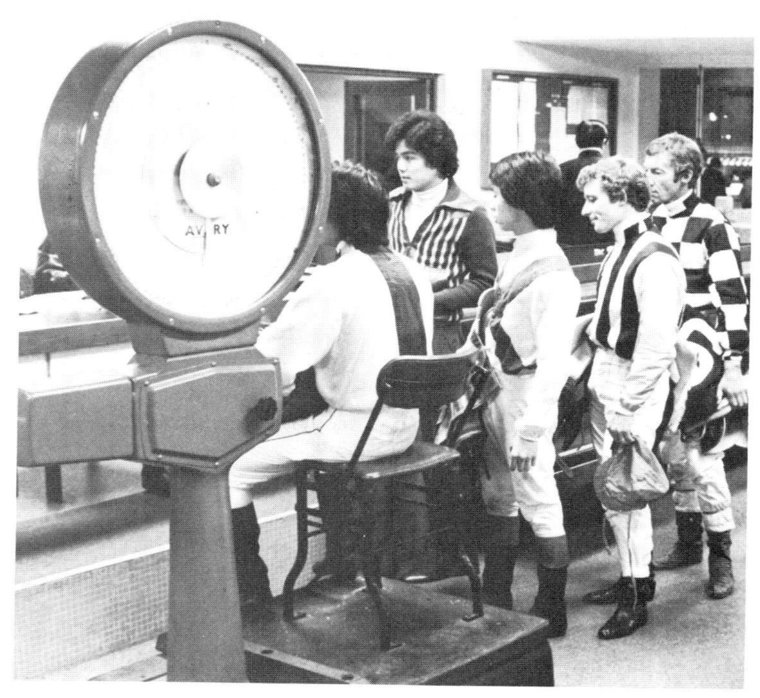

'56 kilos, sir' (8st 11lbs). The problems are the same world-wide. This is Hong Kong, one of the richest racing countries in the world and a regular winter stop-off for Lester.
Gerry Cranham

prize on Steel Pulse, with Roberto, evidently not recovered from his thrashing, twelfth of fourteen.

Three weeks later the Dom Perignon 1966 tasted sweet to the veteran Australian at a private party given by Steel Heart's owner Ravi Tikkoo, at London's Sportsman Club. It was a convivial occasion, but as the evening progressed it became clear to me what remarkable bitterness had built up within this mild-mannered man, against the principals in the Roberto affair. As the story spilled out, much of which I undertook never to repeat, I could understand this honourable man's fury. Sadly, he kept that bitterness until the day he died, a few years later, from cancer. He never was to win the Derby.

Happily, Lester's fourth Derby for Vincent O'Brien on The Minstrel, in 1977, was gained without bitterness or recrimination, except from those who considered his use of the whip to be unacceptably excessive.

The Minstrel, however, unlike Roberto, did not lose his form. His triumph at Epsom, by a neck from Willie Carson on Hot Grove, was followed by equally courageous wins at The Curragh and in the King George. 1977

14

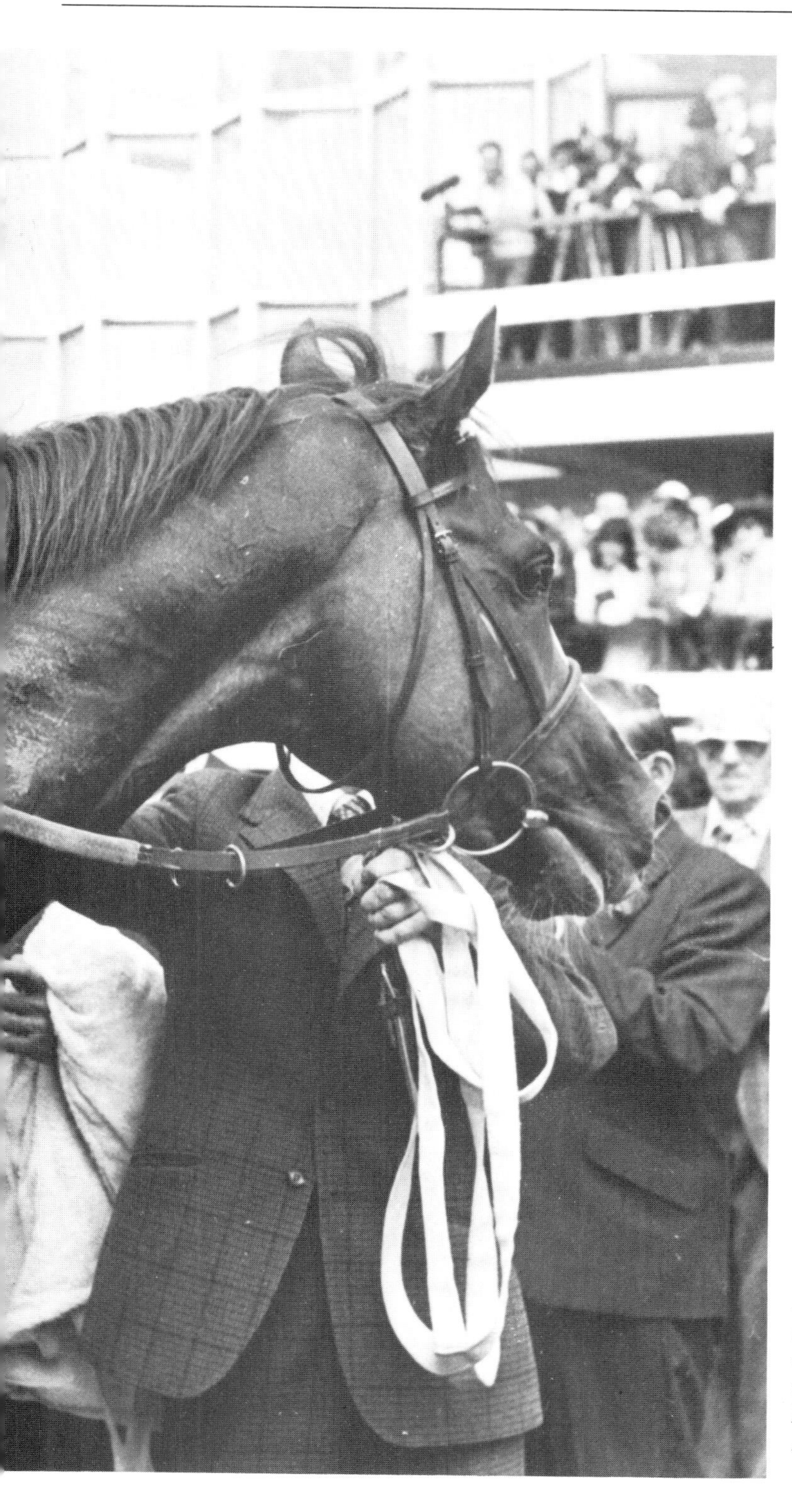

Lester smiles sensation! Lester eyes the diamond prizes after his narrow victory on The Minstrel in the King George VI and Queen Elizabeth Diamond Stakes. It was to be The Minstrel's last race.

Sport & General

was 1970 all over again, with icing on top. The Minstrel's four wins were worth £274,000 and Alleged's Arc de Triomphe £140,845. Lester's seven wins at Royal Ascot included an eighth Gold Cup on Sagaro. It was a vintage year by any standards – though it still took him into only fourth place in the voting for BBC TV's Sports Personality of the Year!

Alleged was the last great horse that Piggott rode for O'Brien. His two winning rides in the Prix de L'Arc de Triomphe in 1977 and 1978 were perfection, and he was the ideal horse for the Arc. He could be ridden close up to the leaders, and he possessed fine acceleration that could be used at any time.

His only defeat in three seasons came in the St Leger, where Piggott's tactics were open to criticism. Lying handy, he found himself in front fully four furlongs from home, with a long wide-open straight in front of him. Willie Carson pounced on the Queen's filly Dunfermline a furlong from home, and although Alleged fought back, the filly's thrust had won the day. Unlike Nijinsky, Alleged possibly benefited from what was his first really tough race; three weeks later he came out to win the Arc without ever looking like getting beaten.

The following season, after training troubles for much of the year, which had the benefit of ensuring that he was a fresh horse, he won again by an even wider margin. He was the first horse since Ribot to win two successive Arcs,, and the jinx that for so long had beset Lester in the Arc was once and for all laid to rest.

THE TWIN TOWERS – THE DERBY AND THE ARC

The challenge of two great races has dominated Lester's fabulous career – the Derby, and the Prix de l'Arc de Triomphe. In the Derby Lester has established a record of successes that will almost certainly never be beaten. The Arc de Triomphe, however, proved so elusive that Lester must have despaired of ever winning it: it took him twenty years to do so.

What was the secret of Lester's phenomenal success in what Disraeli once described as 'the Blue Riband of the Turf'? How could he come to win the race nine times before the age that the twentieth century's other truly great jockey, Sir Gordon Richards, won it for the first time? How could he dominate the race to such a degree that ambitious owners would supercede loyalty to their own stable jockeys, and offer fabulous rewards to Lester to ride their horse in the big race?

The answers lie in the man himself. It was Steve Donoghue, in the twenties, who set the standard by which Derby jockeys came to be judged. Steve, who had scant regard for his stable ties, had a similar attitude to Lester in the acquisition of Derby rides. The Irish charm with which he poached other men's mounts made the process rather more acceptable than Piggott's more laconic approach.

Donoghue won the 1921 Derby on Humorist for Mr J.B. Joel, when retained by Lord Derby, and the 1923 Derby on Papyrus when retained by Lord Woolavington. On each occasion his principal retainer had a runner in the race.

Donoghue shared Piggott's qualities of single-minded determination, and complete lack of fear. The Irishman's prime rule in the Derby was to ensure that he was in the first three round Tattenham Corner. Between 1921 and 1923 he achieved the only hat-trick in the history of the race. On Humorist, he was third round

2

Tattenham Corner, and soon led. On Captain Cuttle and Papyrus he led immediately after Tattenham Corner. He would always, if possible, tack over to the rails, and his left boot would brush the paint on the rail.

It became a method of riding the race that was a millstone to successive generations of jockeys, not least Gordon Richards. Year after year, over anxious jockeys would 'burst' their mounts rushing down Tattenham Hill, leaving nothing in reserve for the rising ground in the closing stages.

Lester, partly through expediency, was to alter the classic standard of race-riding in the Derby. Sir Ivor, Nijinsky, Roberto, Empery and The Minstrel had one thing in common: they were all American bred. In America the 'Classic' distance, the distance of the Kentucky Derby, is a mile-and-a-quarter. For generations the Americans have bred for speed, speed and more speed. So American-breds coming to Europe required a complete mental re-adjustment to become accustomed to the British manner of racing.

The skills of pioneer trainers like Vincent O'Brien, who fastened upon the American yearling market, enabled successive generations of American-breds to relax and adjust. But the die-hards, taking pedigrees at face value, would not accept that these precious imports would be able to stay *Britain*'s Classic distance, over one of the most searching and difficult-to-ride courses in the world. In the case of Sir Ivor and Nijinsky, it was an opinion that cost certain bookmakers very dear.

The Derby course at Epsom is unique. Very few jockeys enjoy riding at Epsom. It certainly was not Gordon Richards' favourite course, while another post-war Champion Jockey was well-known to be terrified of Tattenham Corner. Most French jockeys actually dread riding at Epsom, and only the inimitable Yves St Martin has made any impact, winning the Derby on Relko (1963), and the Oaks on Monade (1962) and Pawneese (1976). Even St Martin, however, does not look forward to the occasion, notably since he became the victim of a toilet roll thrown by a hooligan in the crowd, which garlanded itself frighteningly around him in 1979.

There are many who consider the left-hand, mile and a

OPPOSITE PAGE. TOP:
The memorable climax to a famous year. Alleged wins his first and Lester only his second Prix de l'Arc de Triomphe, from the British trained but now New Zealand bred Balmerino (Ron Hutchison). Alleged suffered only one defeat in his entire career. Ed Byrne

BOTTOM:
'Come on Steve!' In the '20s and '30s the public would support Steve Donaghue (second left) as blindly as they did Piggott in post-war years. Wily Harry Wragg is the jockey on the left.
BBC Hulton Picture Library

half circuit an absurd site on which to run the world's most famous flat race.

The course rises about 150 feet at varying gradients for the first five furlongs, after which it descends until the last 150 yards, which are uphill. The first half mile is especially hard to ride in a large field, as about two furlongs after the start, after a stiff incline, it has a right-hand dog-leg. The field run diagonally towards the outside rail, leaving little room for those drawn on the outside. Those on the inside, meanwhile, tend to lose their place and be chopped off when the field runs back to the left-hand rail a furlong later. In many ways the centre is the best place to be drawn.

The climb continues till almost opposite the seven furlong start. Whereafter the ground drops away increasingly sharply left-handed down to Tattenham Corner, four furlongs from the finish. This is the most frightening period of the race, with early front-runners beginning to drop back, those at the back looking to improve their position, and horses tending to lose their action and get on the 'wrong leg', on this unusual terrain. It was here that six horses fell in 1962, in the worst pile-up in the history of the race.

Once round Tattenham Corner, where many horses tend to run wide, the course continues downhill with an increasing camber towards the far rail, which tends to get tired horses unbalanced. The last 150 yards is rising ground over which the race can be won or lost. In 1984 it

TOP. LEFT:
Aftermath of disaster. Ambulance men tend the injured jockeys after the 1962 Tattenham Hill pile-up, unseen from the stands. For several years the author was positioned by the BBC on the Simon Hoist (background) in case of a similar mishap. Happily the disaster has not been repeated.
Photo Source/Keystone

TOP. RIGHT:
The final hundred yards at Epsom that make or break. From winning on a tight reign, suddenly El Gran Senor (nearest) is at full stretch – and sensationally beaten by Secreto (C. Roche). The defeat supposedly knocked $20 million off his value and the following spring he proved infertile! After the race Lester whispered to trainer O'Brien: 'Do you miss me?' Sport & General

OPPOSITE PAGE:
Poised to pounce. Mitilini (bred by the author) leads Teenoso (Piggott) round Tattenham Corner. As always the Maestro is perfectly placed one off the rail, and already looking for dangers. Sport & General

was lost for the American-bred El Gran Senor, ridden by Pat Eddery, who failed to stay. After the race, which devalued El Gran Senor by up to $20 million, Piggott is said to have whispered in Vincent O'Brien's ear, 'Do you miss me?'!

Lester's great gift at Epsom lies in his skill of getting his horse to relax. In the first two furlongs of the race, where jockeys tend to bustle their horses to get a position, dart for narrow gaps, and generally ride in a stop-go manner, Lester would ensure his mount enjoyed a smooth progress. Over the stiffest part of the ascent, he has the gift to 'switch off', so that his mount expends a minimum amount of energy.

At the top of the hill he would give his mount a breather, to fill their lungs; free-wheel down the start of the descent, and start to ride a race running down Tattenham Hill. He would always track a horse with a winning chance, so as to avoid being knocked back by beaten

The disaster Derby. Six loose horses, including the favourite, Hethersett, at the end of the 1962 Derby tell a tale of havoc at the top of Tattenham Hill. A seventh horse, King Canute II broke his leg. The winner was the white-faced Larkspur, a first Derby triumph for Vincent O'Brien.
Photo Source/Keystone

horses. Somehow, he would always have *room* – whether through an instinctive gift, or latterly simply because he was 'Lester'.

Usually poised one horse away from the rails so as to have two options, Lester would cover up his 'non-staying' mount until two furlongs from home. Then came the decisive thrust, his horse full of resources, perfectly balanced, eased into overdrive for the final burst. Of course, with staying horses like St Paddy and Teenoso, the race was less complicated. On such an animal the Donoghue method was the safest, and most effective.

Lester's other great gift was the ability to evaluate the strengths and weaknesses of all his opponents, human and equine, and to keep his mind totally cool and lucid. While other jockeys were over-revving, adrenalin shooting, 'Mr Cool' would change calmly and relaxedly, his computer brain thinking of people to see, rides to come and probably travel plans for the weekend.

He would always try to be the last man in the starting stalls, and any delay at the start would be an excuse to take the weight off his horse's back. In short, at Epsom, he was a perfectionist, who more often than not achieved perfection.

Lester's pursuit of the Prix de l'Arc de Triomphe was quite the opposite. The Arc is a difficult race to win. It is

'What do you think of it so far, Brough?' Lester reverses roles with ITV inquisitor Brough Scott during the 1983 Derby. A late injury to Simply Great left Lester a spectator for the first time in twenty years.
Topham

The elusive Arc. The brilliant Park Top just fails to catch Levmoss (Bill Williamson) despite a flying finish. Some critics blamed the jockey for the mare's defeat, but in truth it was an impossible race for Piggott to ride.
Photo Source/Central Press

the championship of Europe, run late in the year over a course that has no clearly defined method of riding.

More often than not the British horses challenging for the Arc are over-the-top after a long season, a notable case in point being the mighty Troy. The French Classic horses are rested during July and August, and brought back fresh for an autumn campaign.

In fairness to Lester, I for one, never believed him to lose an Arc that he should have won. On several occasions he rode outstanding horses that were not ideally equipped for the race. But in no respect could it be called his lucky race. Three wins from twenty-seven rides, up to 1984, by his standards is a disappointment. Furthermore, on four occasions he was beaten less than a length – on Ribocco, Park Top, Nijinsky and Ardross. Twice he was banned from riding in the race because of concussion. Ribocco, who had won the St Leger, found the race one hundred yards too short; he was a horse who did things in his own time. Lester rode him with skill and finesse. Sir Ivor met a horse (in Vaguely Noble) who was simply too good; while the charming, charismatic Park Top was another animal who had to be ridden with a velvet glove. Bill Williamson exploited her idiosyncrasies brilliantly, riding Levmoss.

So it was in the wake of sixteen failures that Lester rode Rheingold – the horse that Roberto had edged out in the

The shattering Arc. Sassafras and Yves St Martin (far side) fight back to head Nijinsky in the last few strides. It was the Triple Crown winner's first defeat, and Vincent O'Brien to this day blames Lester for it.
Agence France-Presse

previous year's Derby – in the 1973 Arc. Rheingold was part-owned by Charles St George, and following the Derby, poor Ernie Johnson had been replaced by Piggott at the owners' request, at York the previous year.

For once, Piggott's rapacity had let him down. Following Roberto's lamentable show in the Irish Sweeps Derby, Piggott informed Galbreath and O'Brien that he preferred to ride Rheingold in the Benson and Hedges Gold Cup. Galbreath, furious, after what he considered his generosity following the Derby, arranged for the Panamanian jockey Braulio Baeza to fly to York to ride Roberto. Roberto made every yard of the running, beating not only Rheingold, but also the previously undefeated Brigadier Gerard, with Joe Mercer up.

In 1973, Piggott renewed his partnership with Roberto, winning the Coronation Cup by five lengths. But then Roberto ran lamentably in the King George VI and Queen Elizabeth Stakes, which was to be his last race. O'Brien sent him to York for a repeat bid in the Benson and Hedges, ridden by Piggott, but following an overnight downpour he was withdrawn on the day of the race.

Piggott, meanwhile, pursuaded his friend Charles St George to allow him to ride Rheingold, whom the French champion, Yves St Martin, had already flown over from France to ride. The normally sanguine St Martin was

American John Galbreath receives the Benson and Hedges Trophy after Roberto had created one of the sensations of the '70s – the first defeat of Brigadier Gerard. Piggott, despite the drama at Epsom, now preferred to ride Rheingold – so Galbreath brought the Panamanian Braulio Baeza from America for the ride. Sport & General

more furious than I have ever seen him. The situation was verging on an international incident involving the English and French Jockey Clubs. Rheingold's trainer, Barry Hills, found himself unwillingly and unwittingly at the centre of a hugely embarrassing diplomatic impasse. Finally, to St Martin's disgust, the Stewards decreed that Piggott should ride the horse. Rheingold started at 6-4 on, and finished a soundly beaten third. Such was the background to Piggott's seventeenth attempt at the Arc.

Rheingold had not run since York, and the firm favourite was the magnificent filly Allez France, ridden by St Martin. On Rheingold, Piggott was able to ride the classic Arc race: third into the straight, strike for home – and catch-me-if-you-can. Allez France made her challenge a furlong from home, but Rheingold, at his peak, galloped her into the ground. At last the Arc was Lester's.

Lester rode Alleged in similar fashion. In 1977, on fast ground, he was always in the van, in a modestly-run race. He led into the straight, and was never under threat.

In 1978, the ground was softer, and the pace stronger, and Lester gave the favourite more of a chance. Once in the straight he was soon in front, and won as smoothly as silk. Within weeks of the race he had been syndicated for $13 million.

Unlike the Derby, the Arc does not have a classic riding

Still friends despite everything! A relaxed Yves St Martin at Doncaster, three weeks after Lester on Rheingold had pipped the French Champion on Allez France, in the Arc. Earlier in the season, Lester had highjacked the ride on Rheingold from St Martin at York.
BBC Hulton Picture Library

formula. For a start, the going can vary from good to heavy. The time for the race in 1983 was two minutes, twenty-eight point one seconds; in 1984, two minutes, thirty-nine point one seconds. Secondly, the pace varies from year to year. Whereas in the old days there were always at least two pace-makers, nowadays there is no guarantee of this.

A problem faces those drawn on the wide outside. In France the rules state that a horse lying prominent must run straight for the first two furlongs. So does a jockey jump off, run wide, and edge over after two or three furlongs? Or does he drop out of the back and try to thread through close to the rails?

I believe that Piggott has never ridden a better race in the Arc than on Ardross, on 3 October 1982, but he had to wait until Ardross, a stayer, was ready to go. As with Ribocco, the distance of the race was one hundred yards

too short, with Ardross finishing second.

Such a horse is at a great disadvantage in that the French like to coil up their horses running down the hill with three and a half furlongs left to race, and propel them for home in the short two-and-a-half furlong straight. A stayer, who doesn't quicken immediately, or a filly, like Park Top, who need to be covered up, is liable to get left behind. Ardross was never checked, and was never more than one horse from the rail – Lester's navigation was uncanny.

If Lester were to write an epitaph for his association with the Arc it would probably be, 'You can't go faster than the horse!'

OPPOSITE PAGE:
At last! At the seventeenth attempt Lester cracks his 'bogey' race, riding Rheingold. Club owner and violinist Henry Zeisel is ready to dance a jig. The celebrations went on for forty-eight hours.

Photo Source/Keystone

'HAS HE GOT ANY FRIENDS?'

Most sportsmen are jovial, outgoing individuals, who make friends easily and enjoy each other's company. Lester's personality is quite the reverse. I do not believe I have ever met a man with whom it is harder to establish and maintain a relationship.

On some days, in private, or travelling, he is outgoing, congenial and extremely witty. A day later, a phone call to his house will be met with a sigh, a monosyllable, and an evident desire to terminate the discussion as soon as possible.

Lester has always enjoyed the company of outgoing people. Possibly his best friend in the Jockey's Room was the late Brian Taylor, killed so tragically in December 1984 in a fall at Sha-tin, Hong Kong. Lester was riding in the same race. Taylor was one of the few jockeys not to be in complete awe of Lester. He would mock and mimic the Maestro, and Lester would love it. Taylor could reduce two dozen jockeys to hysterics with his nasal Piggott impersonation.

Occasionally Lester would take a young jockey under his wing, either the son of an old friend, or as a protege to groom as a possible stable jockey. Walter Swinburn, for instance, has always found Lester kind and helpful.

Most of Lester's best friends over the years have been successful men involved with racing. Best known is his friendship with the racehorse owner Charles St George, in some ways a godfather-type figure, with a property in Mayfair, and a £750,000 house and racing stables in Newmarket. St George's business activities include Chairmanship of Oakeley Vaughan Insurance, and underwriting membership of Lloyds; it was he who sponsored Lester's membership of Lloyds.

St George has invariably had between twenty and thirty horses in training in which Lester has maintained a close interest. More than one jockey/trainer relationship

'Where shall we put this one, Susan?' Another award, this time the William Hill Golden Spur. Alongside, apprentice award winner Bryn Crossley, one of the young riders encouraged by Lester. Bob Champion – with a Special Award – has a double handful! Topham

Lester's close friend and mimic Brian Taylor. Of similar height to Piggott, Taylor based his style closely on the Maestro's. Tragically, he was killed in a race fall in Hong Kong in December 1984. Sport & General

has come to an end because of St George's desire that Piggott should ride his best horses. It was on one of St George's most popular horses, the stayer, Ardross, that Piggott rode his 4,000th winner – and one of his finest-ever races – to finish second in the Prix de l'Arc de Triomphe.

At the start of last season, St George's senior trainer was the Newmarket-based Henry Cecil, but even before the season began there were rumblings of concern. The American Steve Cauthen had succeeded Lester as Cecil's stable jockey – but how long would that arrangement suit Lester and St George? St George has great charm, and Lester has always been comfortable with the big and formidable man. His capacity for needling Lester has always kept the jockey amused.

Lester's first close friend in racing was also an owner, Pierre 'Teasie-Weasie' Raymond. Lester and Susan are still frequent guests of Raymond and his beautiful wife Rosalie for Ascot races. Raymond was a substantial backer in the fifties, and owned several successful jumping horses with Keith Piggott. Several of Lester's twenty wins from fifty-six rides over hurdles were for Raymond. Lester's last ride over hurdles was during the 1959-60 season, but in 1966, at the height of his reputation, he was offered £2,000 by Raymond to ride his horse Lanconello in the Champion Hurdle. Lester declined!

Raymond had a streak of ruthlessness that may have rubbed off on an impressionable young man. He certainly didn't discourage Lester's life-long affair with ready cash. His attitude towards jockeys and some trainers was exemplified by the unusual act of replacing the jockey who had won his first Grand National for him the following season. In recent years Raymond has suffered terribly from cancer, which has necessitated drastic surgery to his face and jaw. As with all those close to him who have fallen ill, and met with unhappy times, Lester has proved a good and loyal friend.

Over the past twenty years, Lester has spent most summer Sunday afternoons riding in France, and his closest associate on this circuit has been the egregious twenty-stone-plus Armenian, Souren Vanian. There has been much speculation as to the source of Vanian's

OPPOSITE PAGE:
A topper of a day. Christine St George leads in Ardross after Piggott's tenth Ascot Gold Cup. It was Ardross who gave Lester his 4,000th winner fourteen months later. Sport & General

Charles St George – the 'Blue Bear' – Piggott's closest associate for over twenty years. Tony Murray rode the grey Bruni to success in the 1975 St Leger, but sensing that Piggott would commandeer the ride the following season, Murray switched to riding in France. Sport & General

Pat Buckley, elated but exhausted after winning the Grand National on Ayala for Keith Piggott and 'Teasie Weasie' Raymond. Blamed for a subsequent defeat at Newbury, Buckley was 'sacked' by 'Teasie Weasie' the following season
Photo Source/Keystone

'We've done it!' Pat Buckley on Ayala feels the ecstasy, and John Lawrence (now Oaksey) the agony of the world's greatest steeplechase. Lawrence's mount, Carrickbeg, had led until the last few strides. Keith Piggott and 'Teasie Weasie' were 'on' the winner at 66-1.

Sport & General

substantial wealth; probably 'import, export' in Sudan is the closest definition. Vanian is one of the Middle East's classic 'Mr Fixits'.

Vanian has raced on the French turf for many years, but recently bought the 450 acre Derisley Wood Stud near Newmarket. With colossal energy Vanian re-built, re-seeded and re-furbished the Stud and buildings, so that now it is one of Newmarket's show-piece properties. At the start of 1985 his stallions included the classic horses Posse and Glint of Gold, as well as the Australian champion Blazing Saddles. In addition to stallions worth over £10 million, Vanian has over seventy superbly-bred mares. Derisley Wood is now Vanian's base – but most Sundays he flies to France by private plane, often with Lester as his passenger. Overseas companies connected with Piggott have share-holdings in more than one Derisley Wood Stallion. Like St George, Vanian is charming, and also possessed with colossal drive and energy. Many of the top men in French racing, including François Boutin and Daniel Wildenstein, are his close friends.

Lester's most interesting associate in France was the late Patrice des Moutis, latterly known in French racing

Ayala, 'Teasie Weasie' and Keith Piggott before the 1964 Grand National. Ayala failed to recapture his form of the previous year and, ridden by David Nicholson, fell at The Chair. Topham

circles as 'Monsieur X', following a series of notable racing scandals.

Patrice des Moutis was a handsome, charming, former amateur rider, who, following a distinguished and courageous war, became an up-market illegal bookmaker and commission agent. His clients were rumoured to include the late Prince Aly Khan.

After the war, des Moutis diversified his interests. He played cards, notably Bridge, was an habitue of Paris night clubs, and at the same time built up a wide range of racing contacts, including crooked jockeys and trainers and racecourse spivs.

In 1951, he was entrusted, remarkably, with responsibility for tightening up the Tote operation in Morocco. Within two years a major scandal had erupted concerning misappropriated funds, the outcome of which was that des Moutis was warned off all racecourses in

February 1953. For the next five years des Moutis returned to Paris to work in the insurance company established by his father.

It was in 1958 that des Moutis developed his interest in the Tiercé, France's football pools equivalent in which each weekend over seven million Frenchmen attempt to nominate the first three to finish in the Race of the Day. In the years to come, Monsieur André Carrus, the lynch-pin of the French Tote (Pari-Mutuel Urbain) and inventor of the Tiercé, was to write cheques in favour of des Moutis for many millions of francs. Within months of des Moutis' assault on the Tiercé, the P.M.U. had changed their rules to limit the number of combinations permitted to one individual. Finally, there were two further changes in the rules. So des Moutis, when the occasion was right, enlisted friends, associates and family to place his combinations country-wide.

His professional contacts within racing included the famous trainer François Mathet, Alec Head and Geoff Watson and jockeys Max Garcia, Jean Deforge, Jean Massard, Jean-Claude Desaint – and Lester Piggott.

In 1970, des Moutis launched a specialist racing weekly called *Le Meilleur*, principally a tipping sheet enlisting the opinions of several top jockeys, with Lester Piggott as its 'star' contributor.

Meanwhile, Tiercé scandal continued to pursue des Moutis. It was following his coup on a trotting race, the Prix de Bordeaux at Vincennes in December 1962, that the name 'Monsieur X' was attributed to him.

Using twenty-five collaborators in Lille, Marseille, Lyon and Bordeaux, and staking almost 300,000 fr. (over £25,000), the syndicate won 4,256,000 fr. (over £300,000). A lengthy inquiry into the affair, followed by court proceedings, revealed that twenty-one of des Moutis's collaborators had criminal records. The case dragged on, inhibited by insufficient evidence of fraud, until finally des Moutis was released on appeal with a one-year suspended sentence.

A second scandal erupted following a Tiercé at Auteuil in November 1969. Thirty-seven helpers staked 700,000 fr. and won 5,700,000 fr. Two months later, a further scandal followed the Prix d'Amerique, France's biggest

The ebullient John Banks, who brought considerable colour to the racecourse in the early '70s. His world crumbled after an enquiry into bribery and corruption in April, 1978, following which he was warned off for two years.
BBC Hulton Picture Library

trotting event. The team invested 15,000 fr. and won 720,000 fr. – winnings that were again withheld by the P.M.U.

It was around this period that Lester's friendship with des Moutis and his wife Marie-Thérèse burgeoned. I dined with Lester as the guest of des Moutis at the elegant Ledoyen Restaurant off the Champs Elysées, on 13 October 1973, on the eve of France's top two-year-old race, the Grand Criterium. It was a memorable evening; superb food in a magnificent tall, old-fashioned dining room; discreet piano music; and an amusing, convivial host. The bill was colossal, and des Moutis tipped most generously. He was every inch the elegant, distinguished turfiste.

Less than two months later, on 9 December 1973, there erupted the greatest scandal in the history of the Tiercé. In the Prix Bride Abattue, at Auteuil, no less than fifteen jockeys, including some of the top names in French jumping, were found to have prevented their mounts from giving their true running. To begin with, des Moutis denied involvement. Eventually, his associates were found to have staked 500,000 fr. on combinations, including the correct one, in Marseilles, Toulon and

Paris, winning 5,333,000 fr., which was again withheld by the P.M.U.

There followed the most dramatic investigation in post-war European racing, including threats, violence and gang-land killings. Eventually des Moutis was indicted and sentenced to five years in prison at Fresnes on 20 February 1975. Ironically, on this occasion, des Moutis was not branded as ring-leader of the conspiracy – the charge he faced was merely attempted fraud. He was released on appeal, but his role was never to be fully played out: that autumn he was found shot dead in the grounds of his house in a Paris suburb. It seemed he had shot himself in the head. The racing world knew better. This time Patrice had got in too deep, even for him. Patrice, friend of the small punters, purveyor of Piggott's wisdom through *Le Meilleur*, was dead. He bore a sad epitaph. The selections of 'Monsieur X' in *Le Meilleur* for the Prix Bride Abattue had not included the third horse, Bodensee!

Another relationship that brought Lester close to the gambling fraternity was his friendship with the bookmaker/punter John Banks, an ebullient Glaswegian who made a major impact on British racing in the late sixties and early seventies. Banks was the type of flamboyant personality that illuminates the racing scene like a bright comet.

In 1969 he landed a colossal gamble in the Royal Hunt Cup with his horse Katmandu – ridden by Lester – and delighted in telling the world about it. 'I don't know how much we had on – we're still counting!', he boasted afterwards. Through his successes he bought a substantial country house in Sunninghill near Ascot, where he delighted to entertain racing friends. His purple and white colours became popular and well-known.

The turning point of his career came when the Jockey Club uncovered an improper relationship between Banks and Champion National Hunt Jockey John Francome in 1978. Francome was accused of exchanging confidential information with Banks, encouraging Banks to bet against certain horses that Francome was riding. Francome was suspended for the remainder of the National Hunt season, and Banks 'warned off' the

Turf for two years. Banks's racing career has never fully recovered.

He is typical of those who have enjoyed a close relationship with Lester: entertaining, outgoing and generous. Almost all of Lester's longest-lasting relationships have been with similar individuals.

It has never been Lester's way to go out and make relationships that last. His life-style and world-wide existence are such that inevitably relationships go into cold storage for up to three months at a time.

Nowadays, the individuals with whom he is probably closest friends are Geoffrey and Patricia Wragg, his near-neighbours in Newmarket, and Ben and Moira Hanbury, whose stables are next door to Lester's. Lester enjoys nothing more than to pop in for a chat while others are eating breakfast. While others socialise in the evening, Lester is watching TV, reading the Form Book, or going to bed.

ANATOMY OF A GENIUS

There are those who simply enjoy genius for what it is, and those who crave to analyse it. Probably the most widely asked questions about Lester Piggott are – '*How* does he do it?' and '*Why* does he do it?'. The first is more easily answered than the second.

The qualities that have played the largest part in Lester's success are strength, balance, courage, determination and strategy – though not necessarily in that order! Lester is exceptionally strong, and like most jockeys, extremely fit. A recent survey in America showed that jockeys appeared to be the fittest of all professional sportsmen. Despite riding in a manner that makes him appear to be kneeling on a horse's withers, Lester has a matchless ability to make a horse stretch whilst running dead straight. A lesser rider will tend to alter his centre of gravity whilst riding a finish, and thus get his horse unbalanced.

Lester once explained in a memorable interview with Kenneth Harris in the *Observer*, 'You've got to be holding yourself as still as you can while you're making the right movements. The more control you have of your body, the fewer movements you have to make – but the more muscular effort you need; you need more strength to stand still on one leg than to walk down the street.

'In the finish of a race, as well as keeping your horse balanced, you've got to be doing things with him. You've got to be encouraging the horse – moving your hands forward when his head goes forward, squeezing him with your knees, urging him with your heels, flourishing your whip, maybe giving him a crack, and all this without throwing him off balance – which means not letting yourself be thrown around in the saddle.'

That, in a nutshell, is what strength in the saddle is about. Lester's exceptional height for a jockey has always accentuated the problem of balance. Once asked why he rides with his bottom in the air, Lester replied laconically, 'Well, I've got to put it somewhere, haven't I?' Less tall riders, with shorter legs and fewer problems of wind resistance, have considerably less stress on their muscles.

Lester modestly ascribes his superior strength to superior weight:

'Take a finish between myself and an eight-stoner. If we both do everything right, and the two horses are about the same in what they have got left, I must win because I have that few pounds extra strength.

'My frame is bigger and my arms and legs longer. It stands to reason I must be able to develop more power in a driving finish.'

In many ways the ultimate example of this theory was Lester's success in the 1977 Derby on The Minstrel, from Willie Carson on Hot Grove. But part of the fascination of racing is that no one will ever know for sure that Carson wouldn't have won on The Minstrel!

Lester's balance defies almost all the laws of gravity. He described it to Kenneth Harris thus:

'The horse has its own centre of gravity just behind his shoulders. The jockey also has a centre of gravity – but the jockey can shift his and the horse can't. At every stride the horse's centre of gravity is shifting in relation to the jockey's. Getting a horse balanced means keeping *your* balance, every stride, every second, to suit his.'

His finest hour? Piggott lifts an exhausted, mud-spattered Ribero to a short head success in the 1968 St Leger from Canterbury (Bill Williamson). Using every aid except the whip, Piggott literally kneels on his mount's withers. Sport & General

That, of course, does not describe *how* Lester keeps his balance, when so little of his leg is in direct contact with the saddle. In short, it is an acrobat's trick, developed by a remarkable horseman over many years – and imitated by a lesser man at his peril! One of the greatest criticisms of Lester's ultra-short style is that so many young riders have aped their hero without having the skill or experience to control their horse.

Lester's balancing act can be compared to riding on the Cresta Run. Very often he will straighten a horse, or get him back on the right leg, just by shifting his balance without pulling his horse's mouth – just as a Cresta rider will shift the weight of his shoulders left or right to change direction on the straight. But for all his virtuosity,

Two men worth listening to. Note the attentive expressions of the travelling head lad and assistant trainer as Piggott and Capt. Ryan Price discuss tactics. Note also the pre-restrictions length of Lester's whip which made it difficult to pull through from one hand to the other.
BBC Hulton Picture Library

FOLLOWING PAGES:
A battle royal! The greatest, and the heir to his throne. Piggott and Pat Eddery fight out an epic finish to the Princess Royal Stakes at Ascot in October 1978. Eddery on Trillionaire (right) just holds the edge, but Piggott tries every trick in his repertoire. The verdict: a short head in favour of Eddery.
Gerry Cranham

Lester's style has meant a considerable number of pre-race falls over the years.

The whip has always been a vital part of Lester's armoury, and there is no doubt that at one stage of his career he did use it with undue severity. Nowadays, there are restrictions on the length and width of a whip, but in the old days Lester's was likened to a fishing rod! It was very long, 'a man's whip', with a split leather thong which made it noisier than most. To hit a horse on the wrong spot – for instance, the stifle – is counter-productive. The pain will cause a horse to curl up and become unbalanced. Piggott gradually developed the art of hitting a horse on the precise point of the rump to achieve maximum encouragement and direct propulsion. Very few horses in recent years have been soured by his use of the whip.

His weakness, however, was for many years, a limited ability to pull the stick through from his right hand to his left (largely because of its unwieldy length), and having done so, to use it effectively in his left hand. Until the seventies he looked positively clumsy. The speed and dexterity with which George Moore achieved this manoeuvre merely emphasised Lester's inability to do so.

Lester's courage is another remarkable feature of his durability. It is relatively common to be young and brave, although in youth, 'foolhardy' is often a better description. At forty-nine Lester rode with the same evident lack of fear that he did thirty-five years ago. I say 'evident' lack of fear, because who knows for sure if Lester is genuinely fearless – or simply overcomes any fear that he does feel? (He once said, 'I can honestly say I have never been frightened. If I felt that way, I would give up.' I believe him.) Whichever is true, he goes for the same gaps, as he ever did very rarely snatches up, and never shouts or screams for room in the way that some veterans are liable to do.

In recent years he has suffered three appalling falls, that would have ended the career of a lesser man.

The first was at Epsom on 4 June, 1977. Lester was riding Robert Sangster's filly Durtal in the Oaks. On the downhill canter to the path across the Downs on the way to the start, Durtal took a strong hold and for a moment

looked like galloping across the main road. Lester pulled her towards the rails, but hit the woodwork, breaking his left stirrup iron. By now, Durtal had panicked and was galloping straight for a solid rail in a cul-de-sac. With a broken iron, Lester was helpless as Durtal half-attempted to jump the rail. Lester was thrown and strung up by his right stirrup, while Durtal tried to gallop away. Mercifully Lester was dragged only a few yards, but emerged from the ordeal as shaken as many people had ever seen him. He could have easily been killed. Being Lester, though, he rode in the last two races of the afternoon, winning the last!

His next narrow escape was also at Epsom, on 23 April, 1981. Lester was riding a five-year-old called Winsor Boy in a five-furlong sprint, and was already installed when the drama occurred. Somehow Winsor Boy wriggled under the front of the stalls, taking Lester partly with him. Lester was almost torn apart. His ear, hanging loose, needed several stitches, while the muscles of his back were scraped and wrenched brutally. The wretched Winsor Boy broke his back, and was destroyed.

Lester was described as 'seriously injured'. Yet just six days later he appeared at Ascot, and steered Rabdan, carrying 10st 3lbs, into second place in the Victoria Cup. The following day, frozen by pain-killing injections, he drove out Fairy Footsteps to win the 1,000 Guineas by a neck.

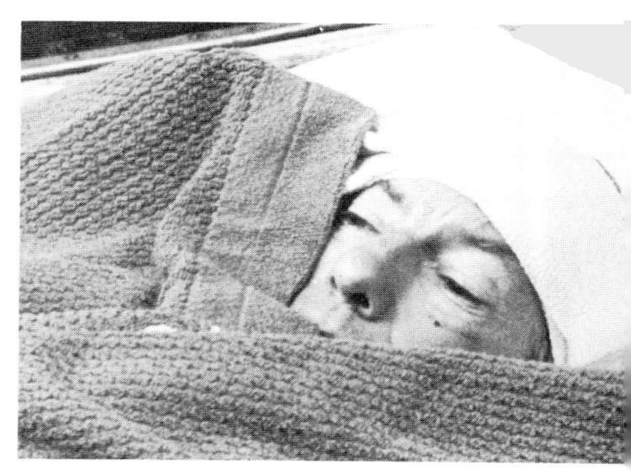

TOP:
Lester Piggott, body aching, measures the margin of success on Fairy Footsteps. Edward Hide's late flourish on Tolmi came too late. It was Lester's twenty-fourth Classic. Sadly, Fairy Footsteps failed to train on, and was retired the following month. Gerry Cranham

BOTTOM:
The end of the road? After a terrifying accident Lester travels from Epsom and District Hospital to Queen Mary's Hospital, Roehampton for plastic surgery to his right ear. One week later he won the 1,000 Guineas on Fairy Footsteps. Press Association

Lester eases into overdrive with Carson to beat. Note the short reign and kneeling posture. While Carson pumps, Lester squeezes.

Gerry Cranham

A slipping saddle leads to a narrow escape for Lester at Brighton in 1960. By a miracle the thundering hooves passed inches by his crumpled body. Sport & General

That was a virtuoso performance, and only once have I seen Lester more emotionally overcome (albeit well concealed) on the racecourse. The occasion was the day of his twenty-eighth Classic success, on Commanche Run at Doncaster in September 1984.

Five weeks earlier, Lester had suffered his most damaging fall since he broke his left leg at Lingfield in 1952. Riding a selling plater called Royal Octave for Ben Hanbury, Lester was starting to pull up while passing the post, when the saddle slipped, dragging Lester with it on the horse's off side. As at Epsom, Lester was 'strung-up' by his right stirrup, and on this occasion dragged almost fifty yards beneath the flailing feet of the frightened two-year-old. After a seemingly endless ordeal, Lester's foot was disentangled, and the eleven-times champion raced to hospital.

Typically, Lester forbade the hospital to issue a comminque and discharged himself overnight. It was, however, an open secret that he had dislodged a small piece of bone in his hip as well as suffering other superficial injuries.

This time, informed 'insiders' really did believe that it could be the end of the line. The York Ebor meeting came and went, the August Bank Holiday passed, and still there was no sign of the indestructible genius declaring himself fit. Finally, on 1 September, he was passed fit to ride at Sandown. Predictably he came back with a winner, the filly Oh So Sharp. But still there were those who felt that he *wasn't* fit and should not be riding, a view enforced by his riding at York the following week. Over the two-day meeting he was beaten on three hot favourites and another strong fancy.

Down, but not out – quite! Anxious arms support Piggott after a heavy fall in June 1977. Ed Byrne

It was then that Lester employed his ruthless determination to secure the mount on the St Leger favourite, Commanche Run. Commanche Run was to be ridden by Luca Cumani's stable jockey, the likeable Darrel McHargue, a top-rated American rider, having his first season in Britain. The horse, however, was owned by a friend of Piggott's, the wealthy Singapore-based owner and trainer Ivan Allan. For two weeks before the big race, Allan was subjected to a barrage of calls from Piggott, climaxed by a cri-de-coeur, 'Listen, you've got to let me ride him, it means a lot to me!'

Three days before the race, the news broke, 'Piggott to ride Commanche Run'.

Darrell McHargue, who had been promised loyalty by an embarrassed Luca Cumani, stated that he would not travel to Doncaster, but would stay at home to play tennis. On the morning of the race, the heavens opened and rain lashed down upon the A1 almost all the way from Newmarket to Doncaster. Lester's driver turned to him and asked, 'Will this rain worry Commanche Run?'

'No', said Lester, 'but it might spoil Darrel McHargue's tennis!'

It is now history that Piggott rode a masterful race to win his record-breaking twenty-eighth Classic by a neck on Commanche Run. As with Roberto's Derby, many said that only Piggott would have won on the horse. We will never know the answer. Sadly, however, Darrel McHargue returned to America for good the following month.

Lester has never complained when the run of the race has gone against him. In recent years, as if by magic, an opening has usually appeared when needed. But it was not always so. Billy Nevett, the former 'Cock of the North', recalls,

'I remember Lester riding Little Cloud for Noel Murless in the 1955 Northumberland Plate. He wasn't much more than a slip of a kid, but the other jockeys gave him the works. I rode in the race and remember he was nearly on the floor three times. He just picked up the horse and went on to win as if nothing had happened!'

The only times I have ever heard Lester complain bitterly have been when he feels he has been deprived of a race that he should have won.

OPPOSITE PAGE:
Oh the relief! The miracle man, torn-ear bandaged, back bruised, lets the mask slip after Fairy Footstep's 1,000 Guineas success. A week earlier he had narrowly escaped death at Epsom. Topham

WELCOME TO DONCASTER
1971
1971

Three notable occasions stick in my mind. First, in the 1968 Great Voltigeur Stakes, when Lester rode a brilliant race on Ribocarre to pip Sandy Barclay on Connaught. The Stewards, however, disqualified Ribocarre for interference, and Lester fumed.

In the 1971 Irish 2,000 Guineas the boot was on the other foot. Lester, on Sparkler, objected to Freddie Head, riding King's Company, for bumping and boring. The two had been at it hammer and tongs, and King's Company won by a head. Lester still feels, 'I was definitely hard done by that day. I did nothing wrong and I got the worst of it all the way. I was on a small horse, and the winner was a pretty big horse, and he just knocked it out of my horse.'

The third and most deeply-held grudge is over Daniel Wildenstein's horse, Vacarme, who was disqualified after the Richmond Stakes at Goodwood in July 1983. Piggott was suspended for 'careless riding'. Piggott will believe till the day he dies that his fearless dart to the rails a furlong from home was justifiable jockeyship. He had an ally in the former Champion Jockey, and recently retired, octogenarian trainer Harry Wragg. 'It was as fine a bit of race-riding as I have ever seen, and as bad a decision by the local Stewards.'

As much as anything it was Lester's strategy and brain-power that kept him ahead of the field. His knowledge of other people's horses is unsurpassed. His exploitation of the weakness of other riders was ruthless. Nothing gave him more pleasure than to pip a rival at the post, turn to him and say, 'You rode like a * * * *!!'

In autumn 1984, televiewers at Ascot saw Willie Carson raise his whip and lash Piggott across the back two strides after the post. Piggott had driven a horse called Prince Crow to beat Carson on Popsi's Joy – a former Piggott mount – by a short head.

'I've beaten you again!' Piggott mocked. Carson cracked. Lester had outpsyched him again. It was a game that he loved to play – and with no one more than the late Brian Taylor. As Taylor would kick for home, believing he had a race won a furlong from home, he would hear a chuckle behind him, 'I'm behind you!' Taylor would panic, and Lester steal the race from under his nose.

OPPOSITE PAGE. TOP:
One short of the record. Lester regales the Press and TV reporters after Circus Plume's Oaks. The tight-lipped era of 'just another race' is light years away. Alan Johnson

BOTTOM:
Athens Wood wins a memorable St Leger under a brilliant ride. Having led from the start, he came under pressure from Lester fully half a mile out, but battled on bravely to hold Homeric and Falkland. After failing to win the following season, he was finally exported to stud in Russia. Sport & General

No justice? An inspired Piggott drives Ribocarre past Connaught (Sandy Barclay) in the 1968 Great Voltigeur Stakes – only to lose the race on an objection by the Stewards. Piggott and Barclay later came to blows. 'I was hard done by,' rued the Maestro. Sport & General

But what devil has kept Lester so insatiably hungry for so long; and what drove him with such ruthless appetite in the first place? For thirty years most people in racing have believed that it is Lester's desire for, and admiration of, material wealth that has been his prime motivating factor. More recently, others have believed that the pursuit of records has been almost as important to him. His will to win, and respect for the rewards of success, is deep-seated, coming as he does from a family of professional jockeys.

His father once said of the Piggotts of his generation, 'If we had a good bet we expected to win. In my younger days, when I was riding, if I had been beaten on a horse that my family had backed heavily and they thought it was my fault, they would not talk to me for a fortnight!'

So Lester has always been single-minded in the pursuit of success, to the exclusion of a normal social life. 'I enjoy the work most of all,' he once said. 'If you like racing more than anything else, it's easier to give up things.'

Lester gave up food, drink, normal social behaviour, and very nearly even normal relationships with animals. Lester never claimed to have an affection for the horses

Lester in the drive position. 'You've got to be holding yourself as still as you can while you're making the right movements.' Lester's balancing act defies close analysis.
Gerry Cranham

'You should see Teenoso!' Underlining that he rides by instinct, Lester drove Teenoso to win the Grand Prix de St Cloud through a haze of blood. Teenoso's head had caused the wound moments before the start. Gerry Cranham

FOLLOWING PAGE, TOP:
Lester lands his sixth Oaks and twenty-seventh Classic in all on Circus Plume hidden by runner up. Out of Shot (right) finished third, but was disqualified for interference and placed last. George Selwyn

BOTTOM:
The record in sight. . .. Lester settles Commanche Run in the early stages of the 1984 St Leger, against the backdrop of the Doncaster stands. Tracking him on the inner is the eventual runner-up, Baynoun (Steve Cauthen).
All-Sport/Trevor Jones

Classic number twenty-nine. The odds-on Shadeed (Lester Piggott), with Lester deputising for the suspended Walter Swinburn, makes heavy weather of beating Bairn and Supreme Leader in the 2,000 Guineas. All-Sport/Trevor Jones

The sensational finish to the 1985 1,000 Guineas. Lester (far side) led to within two strides of the post on Bella Colora – yet finished only third to Oh So Sharp (Steve Cauthen) and Al Bahatri (Tony Murray). Piggott had ridden Oh So Sharp as a two-year-old, and told the author in spring 1985, 'She could be the best filly I've ever ridden'.

Gerry Cranham

'Hold tight Lester!' A rare moment of tension as Lester guides the temperamental Theatrical to post well behind the other runners for his 1985 Derby ride. Gerry Cranham

That's a relief! For once Lester had misjudged the photo finish verdict, and believed he was beaten on Lypharita. In fact the outcome was his third French Oaks success in six years. Gerry Cranham

PREVIOUS PAGE:
'You don't need that, do you?' Lester relieves gateman Joe Smith of his brolly after parting company with Mackelly at Goodwood in August 1977. Mackelly is now a top ladies point-to-pointer. Sport & General

A true Piggott. Note the furrowing features, the family nose, and the jockey's powerful hands and wrists. Lester was born with 'hands', the horseman's gift, but he also has considerable physical strength. Photo Source/Fox

he rode. 'I don't talk to horses,' he once confessed. 'All horses are alike to me. They all obey the same orders.' Nor, until now, has he spent any great period of time studying horses in box or paddock, to develop a close relationship.

Three horses for whom he did develop a soft spot were Primera, Park Top and Moorestyle. Primera was a semi-classic horse, trained by Murless, whose finishing run had to be timed to the second. Once he had struck the front, he had done enough. He went on racing until the age of six, and got better with age. He won the Ormonde Stakes, the Princess of Wales Stakes twice, and the Ebor Handicap, with nine stone.

Park Top was a filly with similar characteristics. Lester's success on her in the King George VI and Queen Elizabeth Stakes was magical to watch. Last, or last but

'I've done you again!' a mocking Piggott on Prince Crow (left) holds off determined Willie Carson on Popsi's Joy by a short head. A split second later Piggott felt the force of Carson's whip across his back!
Alan Johnson

one, coming into Ascot's short straight, she cruised through the field hard on the rails like a knife through butter. Every gap that was needed instantly appeared. In the end, the mare was in front almost too soon!

Lester said at the time, 'She is a great mare and a great character. She knows what she is supposed to do and she loves it. When I get up on her she cocks an ear like she is saying, "Come on then, let's get on with it." She doesn't pull, doesn't sweat, she knows what it's all about. She goes into the gate as if she were going into church, and she comes out as if the Hounds of Hell are after her. She knows more about racing than I do!'

Moorestyle earned a place in Lester's affections for a different reason. He was bought as a yearling by Susan Piggott for just 4,000 guineas, and eventually offered for syndication at a valuation of £2 million. His owners were Moores International Furnishings Ltd., for whom he provided an inexpensive and most successful advertising campaign. He was trained by Susan's brother, Robert Armstrong, and ridden by Lester.

Primera, one of Lester's all-time favourites, after winning the 1959 Ebor under 9st and a virtuoso ride. For once a dehydrated Piggott looks more drained than his mount.
Sport & General

Moorestyle won thirteen races from twenty-one starts, including the Sprint Championship of Europe, and he always ran his heart out. Although Lester would never betray his sentiments with more than a casual pat, he had a real depth of feeling for this almost 'freak' racehorse. Sadly, Moorestyle died after three seasons at the National Stud.

Lester has always been hugely competitive, 'It's not the winning, it's the *wanting* to win that's important', he once said. But why should he drive himself on, when already enjoying multi-millionaire status?

I believe that two episodes in his life had an especially deep-seated effect: first, his suspension in 1954, and second, the robbery from his Newmarket house during September Sales week in 1966. Few people know the truth of that painful experience: not surprisingly Lester has always been loathe to discuss it. I was informed at the time, by a close associate of Lester's, that the sum in question was £70,000. Such a loss would have made him deeply unhappy.

The regal Park Top. Piggott's run on the rails in the King George VI & Queen Elizabeth Stakes looked a miracle at the time, though with his rivals drifting left it can be seen that there was eventually enough room for a double-decker bus!

Sport & General

It raises the intangible subject of how much the former champion has earned. Occasionally statisticians provide helpful estimates. In 1959 it was reported that he had earned £30,000 from rides, retainer and winning percentages. In 1969 it was calculated that he had won £524,243 for his owners in Great Britain and France. A matter of ten per cent of that sum would be a reasonable estimate of his rewards. There would also often be substantial presents from grateful owners, and ad hoc earnings during the winter and spring elsewhere in the world.

Piggott's money has always been well invested, worldwide. He has dealt in bloodstock and breeding companies; share-holdings; gold; property; aviation, and other areas, many of which even he will have forgotten. Only he knows the extent of his present world-wide holdings.

In the seventies he built his impressive Newmarket stable-block and modern luxury bungalow. Even if he fails as a racehorse trainer, his property assets will provide a cushion for the rest of his life. Equally he has laid

'That's my girl.' Daughter Maureen, a regular at Badminton, is now a top name in three-day events. Last spring she jumped the Grand National course in company with ex-jockey commentator Richard Pitman. Topham

the foundations to be able to live abroad in a warmer climate. Lester can have no fear of suffering the fate of many great racing names – ending up old and 'skint'.

What he does fear is failure in the future: he is too used to being a winner.

PIGGOTT LORE – THE MAN AND THE MYTH

A popular way in which to spend an amusing half hour amongst racing folk is to exchange 'Piggott' stories. Invariably, almost all the stories are centred around his legendary meanness. Lester has always played up to this concept in the manner of Jack Benny. Many of the stories are apocryphal. Certainly many are libellous!

Perhaps the most famous is the 'deaf-ear' story which goes as follows. An old stable-man who had 'done' (looked after) a winner that Lester had ridden, was still awaiting, after several weeks, the customary present from the stable jockey. Finally, he plucked up courage to confront Lester.

'Excuse me Lester, but could you see your way to dropping me a pound for that winner I did you?'

'Uh?' muttered Lester, putting on his deaf look.

'Would you give a pound for that winner I did you?' repeated the lad.

'I can't hear,' muttered Lester, 'that's my bad ear.'

The old boy moved round to his other side.

'What about a couple of quid for that winner I did you,' he shouted.

'Can't hear,' replied Lester. 'Try the one-pound ear again!'

Lester has always enjoyed a dry sense of humour, which often manifests itself at the expense of self-important and unknowledgeable owners. Once Lester has ridden a horse, he does not require orders, except in special circumstances. Nor does he suffer fools gladly.

One day in 1958, Lester was in the paddock about to mount the top-class sprinter Right Boy, a horse who as a four-year-old won the Cork and Orrery Stakes, July Cup, King George Stakes, Nunthorpe Stakes and two other races. The horse's owner, an overweight Midlands bookmaker, decided to give his jockey copious and quite unnecessary instructions. Finally Lester's patience

The flying grey Right Boy. Having steered the brilliant sprinter to several major successes, Lester was equivocal towards the owner's insistence on detailed riding instructions. . . ! Sport & General

snapped. 'Listen,' he said. 'If you like I'll take the ******* colours off and you can try!' Collapse of a stout party.

Lester has never been entirely hospitable, at least on the racecourse, to overseas jockeys, ever since the fifties when the rivalry between the French and English was potentially lethal. It was before the days of the camera patrol. Lester had a particular rivalry with Mme. Suzy Volterra's jockey Max Garcia, who, on more than one occasion, had attempted to put Lester over the rails at Longchamp.

One day before a big race at Ascot, Piggott was in the paddock with Noel Murless when the Queen passed by, and paused to wish Piggott and Murless good luck. 'What did she say?' asked the genuinely hard-of-hearing Piggott as the Queen moved on. Quick as a flash, Murless replied, 'She said, she doesn't mind what you do, as long as you leave that bloody Frenchman alone!' Piggott sighed, and shrugged his shoulders. 'All right, if she says so,' he said doubtfully. 'I won't touch him then.' Garcia never had an easier ride in Britain!

The year before George Moore came to England, another top-class Australian jockey in Des Lake arrived in Europe, to ride for the late Paddy Prendergast. Piggott had ridden many winners for Prendergast, but finally the Champion's capricious and extemporaneous conduct became too much for 'P.J.', so Lake was summoned. From the outset, there was no love lost between the two jockeys. On his first visit to England, Lake was advised, 'Watch out for Piggott'. 'Who's he?' replied the Australian. One day soon afterwards, with the rain cascading from the sky, Lake emerged from the Weighing Room, and arrived in the paddock wearing a smart, see-through plastic mackintosh over his colours.

Piggott looked at the Australian with contempt, and muttered:

'That's the first time I've seen a c**t wearing a French Letter!'

Lake lasted for two seasons in Europe, then returned to Australia.

Lester has always held his own in the face of strong animosity abroad, and has never been afraid to take on the locals. In 1952, the late George Cambanis, a member of the Greek Jockey Club, who also had horses in training in England, invited Piggott for a month's working holiday in Athens. It was the period when weight was starting to be a problem for the seventeen-year-old star apprentice, notably in the winter. Cambanis called together the senior local jockeys and appealed, 'Please look after this boy and don't give him a rough time. Remember he is our guest.'

Piggott's first ride was on an apparent no-hoper, which nonetheless led into the short straight. A fancied horse ranged upsides, but surprisingly faltered. The two horses raced neck and neck until the last fifty yards. Finally, the fancied horse drew clear.

'Why did it take you so long to win?' the winning trainer asked his jockey.

'Because that English **** grabbed hold of my ankle, and wouldn't let go!' the local rider exploded.

What by some has been looked upon as meanness over the years, to Lester it may merely have been an amusement. Peter O'Sullevan recalls the aftermath of the 1960 Derby, when he was commissioned to accompany Piggott back to the Lime Grove Studios for a Sportsview inter-

The familiar exodus from a court of law. A brilliant driver, Lester has nonetheless incurred a regular series of fines and disqualifications for speeding. Press Association

Long-time friend Peter O'Sullevan broke the story of Lester's retirement on 19 January. It was O'Sullevan's post-Derby interview with Lester in 1960 that prompted Lester's remark: 'I bet I'm getting more for this than you!' Topham

OPPOSITE PAGE. TOP:
Lester's Away Day. The former Champion values his August weekends at Deauville on the Normandy coast. For years he was a regular at the attractive Hotel du Golf. Gerry Cranham

BOTTOM:
De-briefing. Lester is always a man of few words, especially after a race. Eventually his reticence became an irritation to trainer Henry Cecil. W. Everitt

view. Lester was his usual taciturn self, showing no indication of having won the world's most famous flat race.

Eventually, a laconic smile broke over his face, as he turned to Peter. 'I bet I'm getting more for this than you are!' Suddenly the car was a happier place!

Another day the story is told that Lester had received a roll of banknotes, £500 in all, from a grateful owner, and was happily counting them in his corner of the Dressing Room. A few minutes later another jockey passed by.

'Hey, lend us a fiver – I'm a bit short,' said Lester.

'What about that lot you just collected,' asked the jockey with incredulity.

'Oh, I don't want to break into that', replied Lester.

Travel has always provided an amusing challenge to Lester's financial ingenuity. In going to the races, it is always accepted that the driver pays for the petrol and the passengers provide food, drink and any other requirements. When Lester was driving, invariably the cry went up, 'Hey boys, anyone got a few quid for the petrol – I'm a bit short!'

Taxis and hired cars always provide amusement. One Saturday evening in August, some years ago, we arrived by charter plane in Deauville, and Lester undertook to arrange a car. One by one the other passengers were dropped off and Lester collected twenty francs from each. When we arrived at the Hotel du Golf, I offered

6

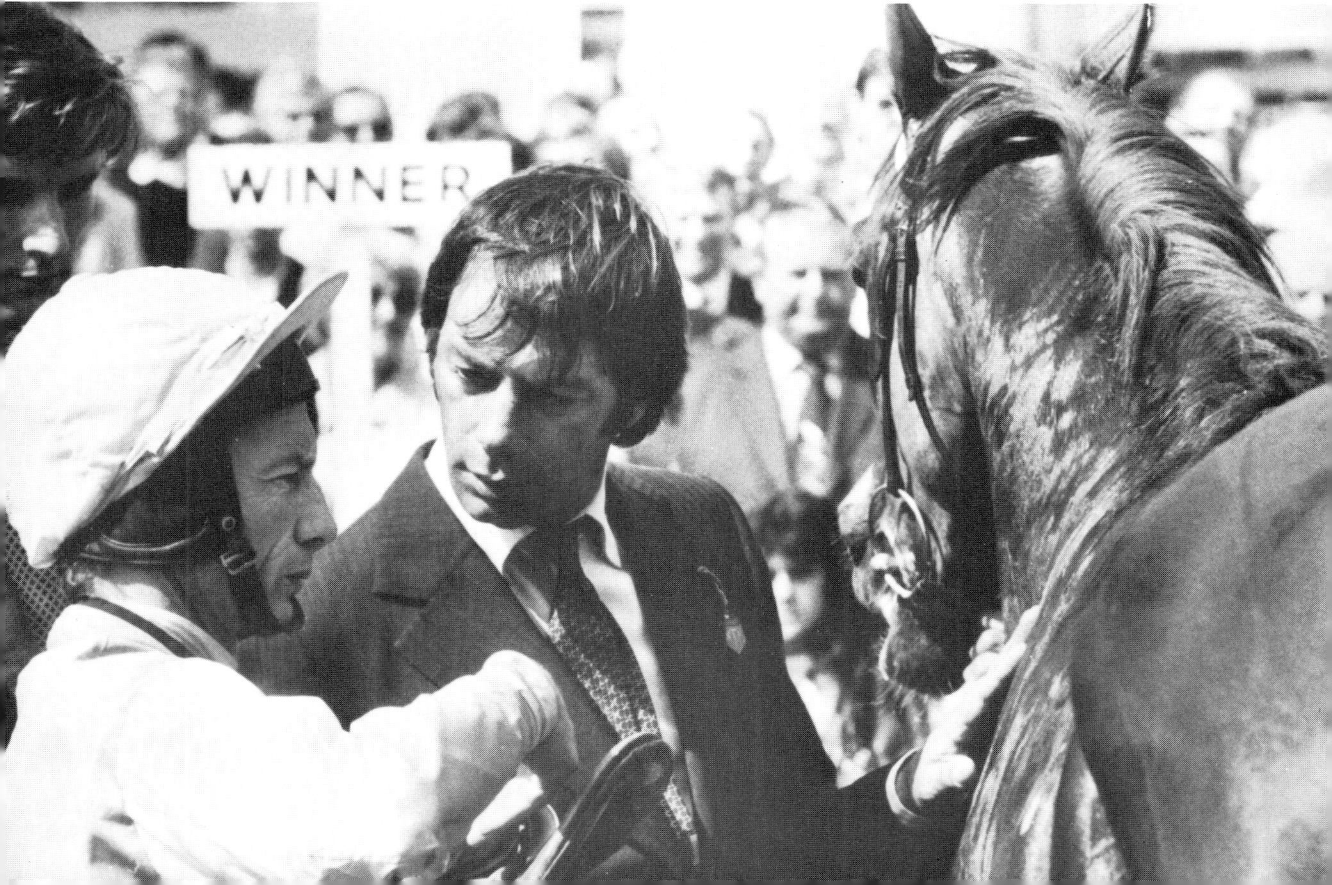
WINNER

Lester my twenty francs. 'It's alright,' he laughed. 'It's already paid for!'

Lester especially resents paying the extortionate parking tariffs at Heathrow's short-term car parks, and has claimed to have devised a method of 'beating the barrier'. From personal experience I know it to be possible!

For all this apparent amorality, Lester is often a thoughtful and caring colleague. If a jockey is injured, it is usually Lester who is the first to visit him in hospital. Over the years he has made a considerable contribution to the work of the Injured Jockeys' Fund and also the Jockeys' Association. Privately, he will help out companions and colleagues who have hit bad times, but hates to be seen to do so lest others should take advantage.

He is a classic 'Jekyll and Hyde' character. At his worst, few people are more charmless and unapproachable. At his best he is amusing and companionable.

In October 1980, while battling for the Jockeys' Title, he rode a two-year-old for some friends and myself at Lingfield. In the paddock he was engaging with my fellow owners – three professional footballers – and after the race, which he won, he chatted briefly, said 'Thank you,' and smiled! The players were mesmerized!

On a bad day, he would have gone through the motions, muttered a monosyllable if one was lucky enough to catch him after the race, and disappeared promptly into the Weighing Room. Sometimes his actions are misinterpreted as meanness, when in fact another element is involved. The Piggotts have no living-in help because they prefer to have the house to themselves. Lester treasures his privacy and total confidentiality. Anyone trying to elicit an indiscreet revelation from Susan very quickly learns he is barking up the wrong tree.

His ability to organise travel is incomparable and he is professionally involved in an aviation service from Stansted Airport. In the Far East, he has been known to re-schedule airline flight times! Whilst in private planes, to any doubting pilot surrounded by fog or heavy cloud, he will invariably say, 'Go on, have a go!'

Some individuals in racing, as previously mentioned, believe that Lester can do no wrong. Others, notably

racehorse trainers 'Snowy' Wainwright and Ben Leigh, have felt that 'enough was enough', and stated, 'Piggott will never ride for me again.'

Piggott's reply, with mock contrition, was, 'Well I'd better pack it in then!'

Wainwright and Leigh are no longer training: Lester is still going strong.

'He'll never ride for me again!' Ben Leigh (left) and Snowy Wainwright (right) each found Lester's unpredictable disregard for riding orders impossible to countenance. Lester's reply on each occasion: 'Well, I'd better pack it in then!'

Bespix

RENAISSANCE – THE CECIL YEARS

4 September, 1980, just two months before his forty-fifth birthday, was one of the unhappier days of Lester Piggott's roller-coaster career. 'Piggott Sacked', screamed the tabloid headlines. Lester had indeed been advised that his contract to ride for Robert Sangster and Vincent O'Brien would not be renewed in 1981. 'Mutual consent' is a much-abused cliche, but there is little doubt that the split came as something of a relief to both parties.

O'Brien, always the perfectionist, was tending to leave his options open more and more until the last minute. Plans would be changed at twenty-four hours' notice. This became increasingly irritating to Lester, who found it impossible to re-arrange his supplementary rides at such short notice. Every week he was letting down trainers at the eleventh hour, and his supply of English rides was drying up.

In 1979 he rode only seventy-seven winners in Britain, his lowest total since 1954. He was 'on the skids' as many saw it, and only trainer Paul Kelleway was offering him consistently good-class rides.

The following year – his last with O'Brien – his career was revived considerably by the patronage of the outstanding young trainer Michael Stoute, who defied the advice of many of those close to him by giving Piggott his 'first rides'. It was a partnership, based on a deep mutual respect, that proved a major unexpected success. Piggott's total of winners rose from seventy-seven to 156, and until the last two weeks of the season he remained a contender for the Jockeys' Title.

But the Sangster split left Piggott without a major contract for 1981. On 7 September, three days after the news from Ballydoyle, Michael Stoute announced that he had retained the brilliant young apprentice Walter Swinburn for the following season. Speculation grew that Piggott, with his own stables to fall back on, would

Bluffing it out. Piggott looks unconcerned as Vacarme passes the post a comfortable winner at Goodwood. But the Stewards found that Vacarme had interfered with Pacific King (white blaze) a furlong from home, disqualified Vacarme and suspended Piggott for careless riding. Few, if any, judgements have upset Lester more. Sport & General

call it a day. As so often in the past, speculation was entirely wrong.

Within five days, a remarkable sequence of Musical Jockeys had been played out. Peter Walwyn – the ebullient Lambourn trainer – had lost his jockey Pat Eddery to Robert Sangster and Vincent O'Brien. For a few days it appeared that the Irish-based Tony Murray would be appointed his successor, but on Sunday, 7 September, came a quite unexpected call to Walwyn from a mutual friend revealing that Joe Mercer would be available.

Mercer, now forty-five, had ridden as first jockey to Henry Cecil since 1977, during which time Cecil had twice been Champion Trainer, and Mercer in 1979 had been Champion Jockey, with 168 winners. It had seemed a perfect partnership. Now Joe was saying publicly that the strain of riding for a Newmarket stable, while his home was in Berkshire, was too great.

What was the true, behind-the-scenes story of what took place before Mercer's resignation, will probably never be fully revealed. What is certain is that one or two of Henry Cecil's owners played a major role. Furthermore, before the Sangster deal was completed, Pat Eddery was approached by Henry Cecil, and Eddery made this known to Joe Mercer.

So suddenly the Champion Trainer was looking for a new stable jockey. Step forward Lester Keith Piggott. By

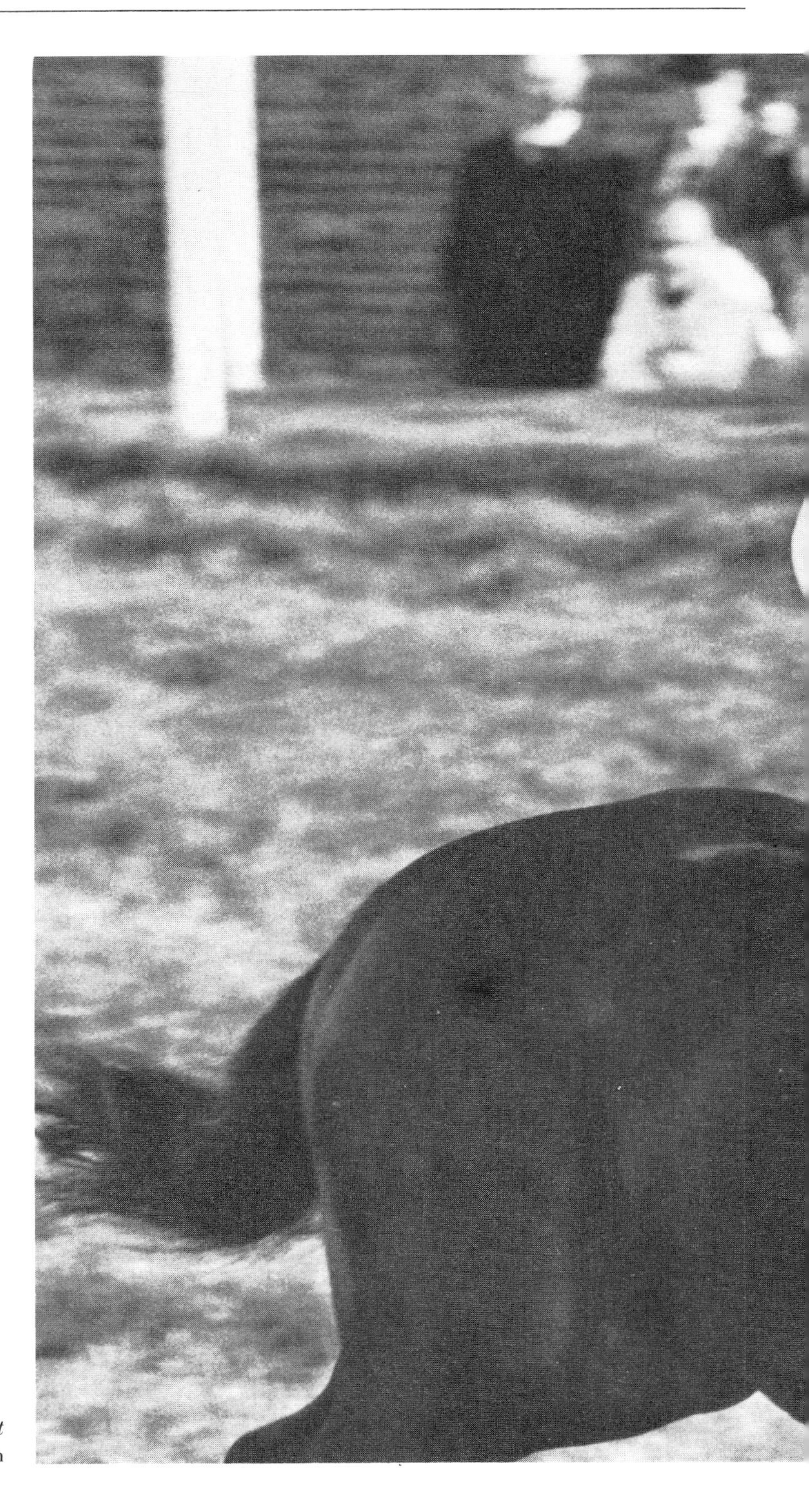

Eleven hundredweight of controlled aggression beneath him up to six times a day. Piggott has always needed terrific muscular strength as well as finesse to make horses do what he wants. Gerry Cranham

Cajun was Henry Cecil's only Group One winning two-year-old in 1981, winning the William Hill Middle Park Stakes at 20-1. On the gallops he was vastly inferior to Simply Great. Sport & General

12 September, within five days of the Mercer-Cecil 'split', the two men had arranged a contract. For Piggott it was a nostalgic return to the Warren Place Stables that he had left in such acrimonious circumstances in 1966. For the mercurial and volatile Cecil it was an arrangement that could lift him to the stars – or explode in his face. In a way it did both.

1981 began on a note of great expectation. Of the older horses there were Ardross, Light Cavalry and Belmont Bay; among the three-year-olds, Gielgud and Age Quod Agis and the brilliant filly Fairy Footsteps; whilst the two-year-olds promised colossal talent.

It was to be a season of ups and downs. Fairy Footsteps won the 1,000 Guineas, but did not race after May.

Furthermore, she was to be Cecil's only Classic runner. Ardross enjoyed a marvellous season, winning the Yorkshire, Ascot and Goodwood Cups, but of the two-year-olds only Cajun won a Group 1 event. Cecil's best two-year-old by far, the unlucky Simply Great, was over the top before the Dewhurst Stakes and ran no sort of race. Nonetheless, thanks largely to Cecil's superb placing of his horses, Piggott became Champion Jockey for the first time since 1971. At forty-six, he was back on top of the tree!

1982 was a triumphant year, despite the accident to Simply Great which quite possibly prevented him from winning the Derby. Cecil was Champion Trainer with record winnings of £872,614, and Piggott again Champion Jockey with *his* biggest total – 188 – since 1966.

Ardross failed by a head to win the Prix de l'Arc de Triomphe, but he, Diesis, Dunbeath, Chalon, Critique, Mr Fluorocarbon and many others put Warren Place firmly back at the top.

For Piggott there was one bizarre episode. The injury to Simply Great left the Champion without a ride in the Derby for the first time since 1962. Instead, he turned TV pundit and viewed from the Stands.

It was in 1983 that the first cracks in the partnership started to show. It began with the controversial disqualification of the 3-1 on shot Vacarme, at Goodwood on 27 July. The Wildenstein family, who owned the horse, claimed that 'Piggott lost the race that was unlosable'. Cecil himself felt that Lester had made his task unnecessarily complicated.

An 'atmosphere' built up between Lester and the Wildensteins that came to a head a fortnight before the Prix de l'Arc de Triomphe. With no Warren Place runner in the Arc Lester was trying to choose between All Along, owned by Wildenstein but trained in France, and the Arab-owned Awaasif, who was trained in Sussex by John Dunlop, and had finished third the previous year. All Along was suited by good going and Awaasif by soft, so Lester was in no hurry to make up his mind.

Something, however, that Lester said to All Along's trainer Patrick Biancone, at Longchamp on 11 September, led Biancone to believe that Lester was

The fateful Arc. Piggott has chosen to ride the Arab-owned Awaasif in place of All Along, thus offending All Along's owner Daniel Wildenstein. Within ten minutes Piggott was to know it was one of the costliest decisions of his life. Topham

It's an ill wind. . . .Lester's decision to ride Awaasif in preference to All Along resulted in fifth-choice Walter Swinburn enjoying the biggest pay-day of his life – ten percent of £228,728! It shows. Selwyn Photos

committing himself to All Along, intelligence that was passed immediately to the Wildensteins.

A week later, when Lester publicly declared that his choice was Awaasif, the tremors could be heard half-way across Europe. 'Piggott gave his word that he would ride our horse', said the Wildensteins. 'He has broken his word, and has not behaved like a gentleman. He will never ride for us again.'

On 24 September, at Ascot, Walter Swinburn was booked for All Along. Eight days later, on an afternoon that Piggott would wish to forget, but never will, All

Along won the first prize of £228,728, by a length. Awaasif finished thirteenth of twenty-six runners.

Many believed that, like dozens before him, Daniel Wildenstein would bury the hatchet: nothing could have been further from the truth. At the start of 1984 he instructed Henry Cecil, who trained twenty-two of his horses, including Simply Great, Legend of France, Claude Monet and Vacarme, that either Steve Cauthen, Walter Swinburn or the best jockey available excepting Piggott, should ride them. It created for Cecil an embarrassing and inconvenient 'two-stable' situation.

Worse was to come. A scandal simmered concerning an unofficial supplementary payments contract, not registered with the Jockey Club, that Cecil had tried to arrange with his owners on Piggott's behalf. The anxiety and tension became acute for the sensitive Cecil. At the end of May 1984, it became too much. An approach was made to Steve Cauthen to ride for the stable in 1985. Cauthen agreed and announced his decision on 5 June.

Piggott, once again, had 'got the sack'.

1985

Lester walked back slowly through the crowds to the weighing room with a wry half-grin on his face. Moments earlier, in his thirty-second Derby, his mount, the Irish colt Theatrical, had finished a distant seventh of fourteen, behind the brilliant winner Slip Anchor. The cheers of the crowd were for the new 'Boy Wonder' Steve Cauthen, the likeable, outgoing 'Kentucky Kid', the young man who had succeeded Lester as Champion Jockey and first jockey to Henry Cecil. How ironic, Lester reflected, that but for the row with Daniel Wildenstein, and the subsequent split with Cecil, it would have been he who returned to acclamation on the new wonder horse.

Worse was to come. Minutes later Henry Cecil appeared on television, and claimed, 'I always thought a lot of him (Slip Anchor) before he ran, but Lester got off him and said: "He's no good!"' 'He didn't have to say that', Lester shrugged on the way home.

From midday the signs had been ominous that it was not to be Lester's day. At 11.15 news came through that the helicopter in which he, Steve Cauthen and Walter Swinburn were to fly was unable to take off from Biggin Hill. A quick telephone call and a dash to the July racecourse produced the offer of a seat in jockey Tony Murray's helicopter. But by 12.40 there was still no sign of *that.* So, after a desperate phone call, Lester returned to where he had started and where Cauthen's helicopter had now arrived. The jockeys arrived at Epsom shortly before the first race. But for Piggott, at least, it was all in vain.

The build-up to the Derby was pure 'Piggott'. In the month following the 2,000 Guineas, his name was linked with at least six horses – Bairn, Damister, Lanfranco, Theatrical, Supreme Leader and Shadeed. One by one they were examined, tried out and eventually eliminated. Within a week of the race Lester was convinced that there

The bitter pill of the 1985 1,000 Guineas. Oh So Sharp (second right), whom Lester had ridden in all her two-year-old races, gets up in the last stride to pip Al Bahatri (Tony Murray) (second left) and Bella Colora (Piggott). Vilikaia is the white-faced filly on the right.

George Selwyn

were only two possible winners: Slip Anchor and Shadeed. Slip Anchor was 'out of bounds', but Shadeed's rider – Walter Swinburn – was suffering from influenza.

Lester had by then agreed to ride Theatrical for the American owner Mr Bert Firestone, but privately Lester made it known that he would swop horses yet again if Shadeed were available. It was all in vain, Swinburn recovered, and Shadeed ran like a 'dead' horse.

A month earlier Shadeed had provided Lester's twenty-ninth Classic success, in the 2,000 Guineas. Originally, Lester had been booked to ride Bairn for the Dubai Sheik, Mohammed al Maktoum. Just three days before the race the unfortunate Walter Swinburn incurred a twenty-one day suspension for reckless riding at the Epsom spring meeting. Shadeed was owned by Sheik Mohammed's brother, Hamdan al Maktoum, and a family conference resolved that Piggott should switch to Shadeed, while Bairn should be ridden by the jockey who was originally due to ride another of Sheik Mohammed's horses, Willie Carson.

Lester sat on Shadeed for the first time two days before the race, and was thrilled by the colt's flowing elastic stride and effortless acceleration. Lester was convinced he was on the Guineas winner. But as so often in racing, there was 'many a slip. . .'. As the runners walked round

Lypharita's last gasp win. 150 yards from the finish, Lester seems to have the £16,000 Prix de Diane (French Oaks) in his grasp. But Freddie Head, on Sitnah, got to within a short head at the line.

Gerry Cranham

the Newmarket paddock on the big day, Shadeed, always keen, began to become irritated and ill-at-ease, throwing out his off-fore leg in evident discomfort. A second lad took hold of his off-side rein to keep him walking straight, in a bid to sooth the high-mettled colt. By the time the parade was due to take place, Shadeed was on the point of boiling over. Trainer Michael Stoute, walking beside his colt in the parade, became increasingly concerned by the manner in which Shadeed was throwing out his off-fore foot, in a way that was clearly a danger to himself.

'Take him down early', Stoute instructed Lester.

It was a decision that led to a fine for Stoute of £550 – and a change in the Jockey Club rules relating to parades! At last the horses were installed and dispatched. Shadeed cruised behind the leader, with Piggott exuding confidence. Three furlongs from home, Shadeed eased to the front, and looked like drawing away. But suddenly the cheers of his supporters became cries of anxiety. A furlong from home Willie Carson launched a challenge on Bairn and Lester became uneasy. From cruising one moment, his mount was suddenly stretching and struggling. Up went Lester's whip hand, and in the final furlong it fell eight times. But Piggott's strength, and Shadeed's courage, were just enough to win the day. Afterwards, almost his first words were, 'He wasn't the same horse I rode on Thursday!'

I suspect that the answer lay in Shadeed's foot. Two weeks before the race, Shadeed was cast in his box, and drove a nail into his foot. For a day or two he was lame, but eventually he was re-shod with a felt pad between his shoe and his foot. On the day of the race the pad was removed, and a light aluminium racing plate fitted. It is my belief that the new plates caused the irritation that made Shadeed behave in such a volatile manner. Whatever the reason, Shadeed was not at his best in the Guineas – and ultimately his success owed not a little to the skills of his rider.

The year had begun in an inconclusive manner. On 19 January, Peter O'Sullevan wrote his final column in the *Daily Express,* and reported that 1985 would definitely be Lester's last year in the saddle. This report and its follow-ups had reverberations around the world, and was then emphatically denied by Piggott for reasons – according to the cynics – not unconnected with certain contractual arrangements with the media!

Soon afterwards, the *Sunday People* published a story that had been hawked around Fleet Street for months, revealing that Henry Cecil had sent letters to some of his owners asking for extra 'cash' payments for Piggott during the period that he was Cecil's stable jockey. Cecil and Piggott, it was reported, had compiled a list of supplementary payments for Piggott in addition to the contract figure officially registered with the Jockey Club secretariat. Piggott's registered retainer for 1981 and 1982 was £10,000, but the terms of the private agreement stipulated that this figure should be increased by a sum rising from £25,000 to £45,000.

Furthermore, Piggott would receive an additional percentage of all prize monies won, and a one fortieth share in any Group 1 winning horse, which was retired to stud anywhere in the world. (Ironically, a share in Slip Anchor immediately after the Derby would have been worth upwards of £1 million on the international market!)

By the time the story was published, Piggott had already faced the wrath of the Inland Revenue. Now it was Cecil who was subjected to the indignity of a Jockey Club inquiry – and on the eve of the Guineas meeting was fined £2,000.

Rather than return to Britain for the cold, damp start to the Flat season on 28 March, Lester predictably delayed his return from Hong Kong and Australia until 3 April. His first rides in Britain were at Salisbury on 13 April. By 1 June he had ridden just seven winners in Britain, while Steve Cauthen was blazing a trail in the Jockeys' Title with fifty-four wins.

Piggott was now riding more and more in France. In Britain all the top stables had retained jockeys and only illness or suspension was making top-class horses available. It was 1980 over again, but more so. The announcement of his retirement seemed inevitable.

Lester showered and changed quietly as the exultant Steve Cauthen ran the gauntlet of congratulations all round, TV interviews, an audience with The Queen, and three more rides after the Derby. It was a routine that Lester had enjoyed many times before. Now, in Steve's hour of glory, almost no one took any notice of the forty-nine-year-old ex-Champion with the pale, tortured face, sitting privately in the corner of the dressing room.

Long before the last race he slipped away quietly, ignoring the good natured calls, 'Give us a tip Lester!' Why on earth, he reflected, not for the first time, should they expect anything from me? I get up, perhaps as early as 5 a.m.; drive up to a hundred miles to ride work, miss breakfast, spend an hour on the telephone after countless hours in the form book. I organise, I orchestrate, and then with a body often wracked with pain I squeeze the last ounce of effort from a tired or reluctant horse. And they expect me to tell them something for nothing?

Three days later, Lester's wry grin became a full-throated chuckle. The *Daily Mail* headlines blazed, 'Wildenstein Severs Cecil Connection'.

'I wonder if he's sending his horses to Lester?', asked one Newmarket wag.

THE FUTURE

Royal Ascot without Lester Piggott will be like *The Third Man* without Harry Lime. It will probably take several years to sink in that he is no longer there.

He will leave the race-riding scene with a career record that will almost certainly never be equalled while racing continues as we know it. His number of winning rides in Britain and Jockeys' Championships is, in each case less than those of Sir Gordon Richards – Gordon won 4,870 races with twenty-six titles, and a best-ever season of 269. But while Gordon rode a limited number of winners abroad, Lester's overseas winners carry his overall total to well in excess of 5,000.

Unlike Gordon, Lester has never managed to 'go through the card' – that is to say, ride all six winners on a programme. He rode five winners at Pontefract on 19 July, 1963; at Leicester on 19, July 1966; at York on 16 August, 1966; at Warwick on 5 September 1966; and at The Curragh (from five rides) on 6 September, 1975.

He has won a race on every British racecourse, and unlike Gordon, rode twenty winners under National Hunt Rules.

He has the distinction of riding the shortest-priced winner ever on record anywhere in the world. When Dragon Blood, ridden by Piggott, won the Premio Naviglio in Milan on 1 June, 1967, he was returned at 10,000-1 on!

It is in the Classic field that Lester's record is exceptional. Leaving aside his many overseas triumphs, his record established in September 1984, of twenty-eight (now twenty-nine) British Classic wins, is one that is surely unbeatable. Gordon's total was fourteen, of which six were war-time substitutes.

He has also achieved the most substantial earnings of any jockey in history, which inflation-linked will almost certainly never be surpassed.

Lester's 5ft 7 ½ ins frame is all muscle and sinew. Like several jockeys, notably Charlie Smirke and Frank Durr, Lester could probably have earned a living in the boxing ring. All-Sport

OPPOSITE PAGE. TOP:
Derby number nine. . . . Teenoso gallops throught the mud to beat the white-faced Carlingford Castle by three lengths. Note the battle royal between the two Sangster runners – the grey Shearwalk and Salmon Leap – for third place. All-Sport

BOTTOM:
'You've probably never seen one of these. . . !' On a recent visit to Lester's house the author counted thirteen Ritz Trophies all in the same cupboard. Ed Byrne

'Steady Susan!' Christmas 1966 at the Southern Cross Fountain, Melbourne. On the eve of the Caulfield Cup, Susan tossed a coin in the fountain and made a wish. Legend has it that Lester popped back to collect it later. . . .
Photo Source/Central Press

Only Gordon, and the tragic Fred Archer, who committed suicide at the age of twenty-nine, can be spoken of in the same breath. Lester Piggott, O.B.E. is an international legend.

But how successful will he be in his future career as a trainer? How easy will he find the switch from 'Glory Boy' to Architect? Lester has two main advantages. Firstly, he grew up in a racing stable, so understands stable-craft and stable routine. Secondly, he has had the benefit of watching two of the great horse masters of our time, Vincent O'Brien and Sir Noel Murless, at close quarters. How much Lester was watching what they were doing, as opposed to what was happening, only he knows.

A further advantage is the influence of his wife Susan, who has run an extremely successful Bloodstock Agency for twelve years. Expert in buying, selling and management, Susan has all the expertise to be a racehorse trainer in her own right.

Lester also has a perfect site, with access to the finest gallops in Europe; the financial wherewithal to acquire the best staff; and owners who will send him any number of top-class horses.

Despite his deafness, he is a good listener, at least to anyone whose opinion he values. The main question marks lie in whether he can communicate with his staff, and whether he will possess the patience that any great trainer needs. He will also be expected to acquire a trilby hat, an accoutrement I have never seen him wear!

Sir Gordon enjoyed reasonable success as a trainer, without approaching Championship status. Only Harry Wragg, of all the Champion Jockeys this century, has enjoyed as much success as a trainer as he did as a jockey. The reason, in a nutshell, was his brilliant strategy.

How easy it will be for a jockey to ride for Lester, remains to be seen. It certainly will not be easy for Lester to find one half as good as himself.

STATISTICAL RECORDS

PIGGOTT'S DOMESTIC RIDING RECORD (GREAT BRITAIN)

1948–84

	1sts	2nds	3rds	Unpl	Mounts	Pos
1948	1	2	0	21	24	–
1949	6	8	10	96	120	–
1950	52	45	39	268	404	11th
1951	51	36	40	305	432	13th
1952	79	47	70	424	620	5th
1953	41	32	45	323	441	15th
1954	42	38	30	152	262	18th
1955	103	84	77	266	530	3rd
1956	129	79	75	359	642	3rd
1957	122	92	83	280	577	3rd
1958	83	81	64	309	537	6th
1959	142	96	85	236	559	3rd
1960	*170*	*107*	*75*	*288*	*640*	*1st*
1961	164	108	73	358	703	2nd
1962	96	77	50	235	458	4th
1963	175	109	71	302	657	2nd
1964	*140*	*106*	*70*	*310*	*626*	*1st*
1965	*160*	*110*	*81*	*304*	*655*	*1st*
1966	*191*	*89*	*101*	*301*	*682*	*1st*
1967	*117*	*100*	*64*	*276*	*557*	*1st*
1968	*139*	*98*	*75*	*268*	*580*	*1st*
1969	*163*	*95*	*87*	*255*	*600*	*1st*
1970	*162*	*110*	*68*	*246*	*586*	*1st*
1971	*162*	*120*	*89*	*259*	*630*	*1st*
1972	103	69	74	218	464	4th
1973	129	80	58	216	483	2nd
1974	143	91	73	279	586	2nd
1975	113	88	61	265	527	3rd
1976	87	68	51	196	402	7th
1977	103	82	62	265	512	4th
1978	97	78	61	249	485	5th
1979	77	54	40	232	403	6th
1980	156	96	65	318	635	2nd
1981	*179*	*113*	*87*	*324*	*703*	*1st*
1982	*188*	*87*	*94*	*329*	*698*	*1st*
1983	150	109	64	318	641	2nd
1984	100	79	72	240	491	3rd
	4315	2963	2384	9890	19552	

11 times Champion Jockey 6 times Runner-up 6 times Third 3 times Fourth

COMPILED BY NEAL R. WILKINS

PIGGOTT'S DERBY RIDES		
1951	Zucchero	left start
1952	Gay Time	2nd
1953	Prince Charlemagne	unpl
1954	*Never Say Die*	*1st*
1955	Windsor Sun	unpl
1956	Affiliation Order	unpl
1957	*Crepello*	*1st*
1958	Boccaccio	unpl
1959	Carnoustie	6th
1960	*St Paddy*	*1st*
1961	(No ride; his mount Pinturischio was doped)	
1962	(Suspended)	
1963	Corpora	5th
1964	Sweet Moss	unpl
1965	Meadow Court	2nd
1966	Right Noble	unpl
1967	Ribocco	2nd
1968	*Sir Ivor*	*1st*
1969	Ribofilio	5th
1970	*Nijinsky*	*1st*
1971	The Parson	6th
1972	*Roberto*	*1st*
1973	Cavo Doro	2nd
1974	Arthurian	unpl
1975	Bruni	unpl
1976	*Empery*	*1st*
1977	*The Minstrel*	*1st*
1978	Inkerman	unpl
1979	Milford	unpl
1980	Monteverdi	unpl
1981	Shotgun	4th
1982	No ride	
1983	*Teenoso*	*1st*
1984	Alphabatim	5th
1985	Theatrical	unpl

Jem Robinson 6 wins

1817	Azor
1824	Cedric
1825	Middleton
1827	Mameluke
1828	Cadland
1836	Bay Middleton

Steve Donoghue 6 wins

1915	Pommern
1917	Gay Crusader
1921	Humorist
1922	Captain Cuttle
1923	Papyrus
1925	Manna

PIGGOTT'S FRENCH WINNERS

1955	1	1960	1	1965	7	1970	43	1975	27	1980	5
1956	0	1961	0	1966	9	1971	18	1976	24	1981	11
1957	0	1962	0	1967	8	1972	29	1977	5	1982	13
1958	0	1963	1	1968	6	1973	18	1978	8	1983	9
1959	0	1964	5	1969	31	1974	22	1979	5	1984	7

PIGGOTT'S OVERSEAS CLASSIC WINS

IRELAND

1,000 GUINEAS
1971 FAVOLETTA
1979 GODETIA

2,000 GUINEAS
1970 DECIES
1978 JAAZEIRO

DERBY
1965 MEADOW COURT
1967 RIBOCCO
1968 RIBERO
1977 THE MINSTREL
1981 SHERGAR

OAKS
1970 SANTA TINA
1975 JULIETTE MARNY
1979 GODETIA

ST LEGER
1967 DAN KANO
1975 CAUCASUS
1976 MENEVAL

FRANCE

1,000 GUINEAS (Poule d'Essai des Pouliches)
1964 RAJPUT PRINCESS
1982 RIVER LADY

DERBY (Prix du Jockey Club)
1972 HARD TO BEAT

OAKS (Prix de Diane)
1980 MRS PENNY
1981 MADAM GAY
1985 LYPHARITA

ST LEGER (Prix Royal Oak)
1981 ARDROSS

GERMANY

DERBY (Grosser Preis Von Berlin)
1957 ORSINI
1963 FANFAR
1967 LUCIANO

OAKS (Preis der Diana)
1967 ON DIT

ITALY

DERBY
1969 BONCONTE DI MONTEFELTRO
1973 CERRETO
1984 WELNOR

1,000 GUINEAS (Premio Regina Elena)
1974 GRANDE NUBE

SPAIN

DERBY (Premio Villapadierna)
1967 MASPALOMAS

OAKS
1972 DELFICA

SWEDEN

DERBY
1958 FLYING FRIENDSHIP

ST LEGER
1982 KANSAS

INDIAN

DERBY (Calcutta)
1968 FAIR HAVEN

AUSTRALIA

OAKS
1985 CENTAUREA

PIGGOTT'S DOMESTIC CLASSIC WINS

1,000 GUINEAS
1970 HUMBLE DUTY
1981 FAIRY FOOTSTEPS

2,000 GUINEAS
1957 CREPELLO
1968 SIR IVOR
1970 NIJINSKY
1985 SHADEED

DERBY
1954 NEVER SAY DIE
1957 CREPELLO
1960 ST PADDY
1968 SIR IVOR
1970 NIJINSKY
1972 ROBERTO
1976 EMPERY
1977 THE MINSTREL
1983 TEENOSO

OAKS
1957 CAROZZA
1959 PETIT ETOILE
1966 VALORIS
1975 JULIETTE MARNY
1981 BLUE WIND
1984 CIRCUS PLUME

ST LEGER
1960 ST PADDY
1961 AURELIUS
1967 RIBOCCO
1968 RIBERO
1971 NIJINSKY
1971 ATHENS WOOD
1972 BOUCHER
1984 COMMANCHE RUN

PIGGOTT'S ARC RIDES

Year	Horse	Result
1952	Oise	unpl
1953	Zucchero	unpl
1954	–	
1955	Elopement	unpl
1956	–	
1957	Prince Taj	4th
1958	Nogaro II	unpl
1959	Primera	5th
1960	–	
1961	Just Great	unpl
1962	Aurelius	unpl
1963	–	
1964	(concussed)	
1965	Meadow Court	unpl
1966	Aunt Edith	unpl
1967	Ribocco	3rd
1968	Sir Ivor	2nd
1969	Park Top	2nd
1970	Nijinsky	2nd
1971	Hallez	5th
1972	Hard To Beat	unpl
1973	*Rheingold*	*1st*
1974	Mississipian	unpl
1975	Duke of Marmelade	unpl
1976	Bruni	5th
1977	*Alleged*	*1st*
1978	*Alleged*	*1st*
1979	Trillion	5th
1980	Glenorum	unpl
1981	Ardross	unpl
1982	Ardross	2nd
1983	Awaasif (c/f All Along)	unpl
1984	(concussed)	

RIDING RECORDS IN THE CLASSICS

Jockey	1st Classic Winner	2,000 Gns	1,000 Gns	Derby	Oaks	St Leger	Total
L. Piggott	1954	4	2	9	6	8	29
F. Buckle	1792	5	6	5	9	2	27
J. Robinson	1817	9	5	6	2	2	24
F. Archer	1874	4	2	5	4	6	21
J. Watts	1883	2	4	4	4	5	19
W. Scott	1821	3	0	4	3	9	19
J. Day	1826	4	5	0	5	2	16
G. Fordham	1859	3	7	1	5	0	16
J. Childs	1912	2	2	3	4	4	15
F. Butler	1843	2	2	2	6	2	14
S. Donoghue	1915	3	1	6	2	2	14
E.C. Elliot	1923	5	4	3	2	0	14
G. Richards	1930	3	3	1	2	5	14
W. Clift	1793	2	2	5	2	2	13
T. Cannon	1866	4	3	1	4	1	13
H. Wragg	1928	1	3	3	4	2	13

Years	
1948–1954	Apprentice to K. Piggott
1955–66	N. Murless
1967–74	Freelance
1975–76	Arrangement – M.V. O'Brien
1977–80	Contract Robert Sangster
1981–84	H. Cecil

Piggott's Championship Years

1960
1964–71
1981
1982

INDEX

Page numbers in *italics* indicate the inclusion of illustrations

E

F

G

H

I

J

K

L

M